Ready, Steady, Party

cooking for kids and with kids

Lucy Broadhurst

MURDOCH BOOKS

contents

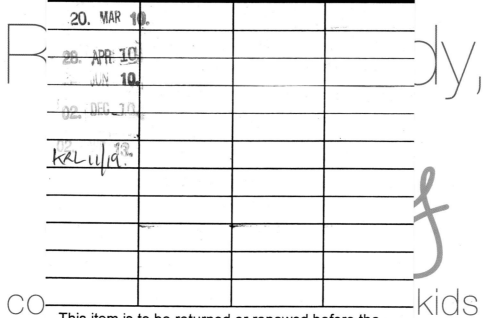

Warwickshire County Council

20. MAR 10.			
28. APR. 10			
JUN 10.			
02. DEC 10.			
02 KRL 11/19.			

This item is to be returned or renewed before the
latest date above. It may be borrowed for a further
period if not in demand. **To renew your books:**

- **Phone the 24/7 Renewal Line 01926 499273 or**
- **Visit www.warwickshire.gov.uk/libraries**

Discover • Imagine• Learn • *with libraries*

Warwickshire
County Council

Working for Warwickshire

read this first...

So you're going to have a party… well there are a few things you'll need to plan before the big day. If you're organised, it will help make your party the best one ever. There are some basic things you'll need to decide. Choose a theme for your party. This is a good starting point and will help you choose what food to make and serve and what kind of decorations you'll need. You will also need to decide if your guests need to wear fancy dress.

Firstly, work out how many guests you want to invite and make a guest list. You might want to have just a few of your closest friends, or perhaps your entire school class! This will also depend on where you are having your party. At home, or a local park, the zoo or the beach? There are so many options and having a theme will make it easier to plan. But remember, if you are having your party outside, make sure you have a back-up plan in case it rains.

Now you'll have to pick the date and time. Make sure the date gives enough notice for your guests. You can't invite people to a party the day before! Two weeks is usually plenty of notice. And make sure you decide on a start and finish time.

Now the fun part… choosing the food you will make. We've divided the book into themes so it's really easy to pick the food you want to serve. Just make sure to find out if any of your guests are vegetarian or have food allergies. Make a list of the ingredients you'll need to buy. Also, see what can be made one or two days before your party, to help save a bit of time on the day. And don't forget the birthday cake!

Organise some games to play at the party. We've got some great games on pages 184–187. Make sure you have everything you need ahead of time. And wherever you decide to hold your party, make sure there is plenty of room for games and running around.

To help you get organised before the party, you might need to make two lists: 'Things to Buy' and 'Things to Do'. Try to do as much on the lists ahead of time as possible so there isn't a last-minute panic on the day of the party. Put the lists in a place where everyone can see it, like on the fridge. This will help everyone remember what needs to be done before the big day.

When organising invitations, decide if you want to make your own or buy them (you can find some great ones in newsagents and party supply stores). You'll need to send or give them out at least two weeks before the party. The invitations will need to have the following information:

- Whose party it is, and what the party is for (for example, Connor's Halloween Party, or Claudia's 5th Birthday Party)

- The day, date and start time of the party, and also including a pick-up time (Saturday 11th February, 2pm-5pm)

- The address of the party, including a map or any special directions if it's difficult to find

- A phone number and email address so your guests can let you know if they are coming or not

- Special information like if it's fancy dress (for example, if you are having a *Shipwrecked* party, let your guests know they should come in costume as pirates, sailors, mermaids, sharks etc). Give your guests as much information as possible about your party theme so they know what to wear.

Next, it's on to decorating your party, which can be lots of fun! Choose colours that suit your party theme. So, for example, if you are having a *Fairy Princess Tea Party* choose pink and purple streamers and balloons. You can make signs that go with your theme. For example, if you are having an *Into The Wild* party, you can make signs that say 'Danger! Lions on the loose!' and 'Watch out for wild rhinos!'.

Safety tips for grown-ups

1 Have a first aid kit handy for scrapes and cuts.

2 Check if any guests attending have serious food allergies. If there is someone attending who, for example, has a severe nut allergy, make sure there are NO foods containing nuts served at the party.

3 Remove toothpicks from food before serving to children under five.

4 Do not serve nuts or small sweets to children under five.

5 Supervise games closely and remove any pieces of burst balloon.

6 If you are having a pool party, make sure there are enough adults supervising the pool and never leave the pool unattended.

7 Make sure parents who are dropping off their children leave contact numbers.

shipwrecked

sailors' knots

MAKES ABOUT 24

1 sheet ready-rolled puff pastry

1 egg, beaten

20 g (¾ oz) grated cheddar cheese

1 tablespoon sesame seeds

1 Preheat the oven to 210°C (415°F/Gas 6–7). Brush a baking tray with oil.

2 Cut the pastry sheet in half, then across the width into 2 cm (¾ inch) strips.

3 Tie each of the strips into simple knots. Place onto the baking tray.

4 Brush the pastry lightly with beaten egg and sprinkle with the cheese and sesame seeds.

5 Bake for 10 minutes, or until puffed and golden. Cool on a wire rack.

Note: These can be prepared up to 3 days in advance. Store in an airtight container in a cool, dry place.

pirates' punch

SERVES 6–8

10 strawberries, chopped

½ pineapple, peeled and chopped

2 oranges, peeled and segmented

500 ml (17 fl oz/2 cups) pineapple juice

500 ml (17 fl oz/2 cups) dry ginger ale

500 ml (17 fl oz/2 cups) lemonade

2 tablespoons chopped mint leaves

1   Combine the strawberries, pineapple and oranges in a large punch bowl.

2   Add the pineapple juice, dry ginger ale and lemonade and stir gently to combine. Stir in the mint leaves and serve. You can ladle into glasses or let party guests help themselves.

Note: You can change the fruit depending on the season. Try peaches, mangoes and blueberries.

sunken subs

MAKES 8

4 hot dog rolls

20 g (³/₄ oz) butter

1 garlic clove, crushed

440 g (15¹/₂ oz) tinned spaghetti in tomato and cheese sauce

80 g (2³/₄ oz) sliced ham, chopped

100 g (3¹/₂ oz) cheddar cheese slices, cut into strips

1 Preheat the oven to 180°C (350°F/Gas 4). Brush a baking tray with oil.

2 Cut the hot dog rolls in half horizontally. Place on the baking tray.

3 Heat the butter in a saucepan. Add the garlic and cook for 2–3 minutes. Brush a little on each roll half. Top with spaghetti, ham and cheese.

4 Bake for 12 minutes, or until the cheese melts.

ham and pineapple pizza wheels

MAKES 16

250 g (9 oz/2 cups) self-raising flour

40 g (1¹/₂ oz) butter, chopped

125 ml (4 fl oz/¹/₂ cup) milk

90 g (3¹/₄ oz/¹/₃ cup) tomato paste (concentrated purée)

2 small onions, finely chopped

4 pineapple slices, finely chopped

200 g (7 oz) sliced ham, shredded

80 g (2³/₄ oz) cheddar cheese, grated

2 tablespoons finely chopped flat-leaf (Italian) parsley

1 Preheat the oven to 180°C (350°F/Gas 4). Brush two baking trays with oil.

2 Sift the flour into a bowl. Rub in the butter using your fingers. Make a well in the centre and add almost all the milk. Mix until the mixture comes together in beads. Gather into a ball and turn out onto a lightly floured surface.

3 Divide the dough in half. Roll out each half on baking paper to make a 20 x 30 cm (8 x 12 inch) rectangle, about 5 mm (¹/₄ inch) thick. Spread the tomato paste over each rectangle, leaving a 1 cm (¹/₂ inch) border.

4 Mix the onion, pineapple, ham, cheddar and parsley together. Spread over the tomato paste, leaving a 2 cm (³/₄ inch) border. Roll up each rectangle along the long edge.

5 Cut each roll into eight even slices. Place the slices on the baking trays. Bake for 20 minutes, or until golden.

mini fishermen's burgers

MAKES 6

6 fish fingers

3 bacon slices, cut in half

6 small lettuce leaves

6 small dinner rolls, cut in half

3 cheese slices, cut in half

1½ tablespoons mayonnaise

1 Preheat the oven to 180°C (350°F/Gas 4). Brush a baking tray with oil. Wrap each fish finger in a piece of bacon. Place on a baking tray and bake for 15 minutes.

2 Place a lettuce leaf on the bottom of each roll. Top with the cheese, a fish finger, then a teaspoon of mayonnaise. Finish with a roll top.

fishy nuggets

MAKES 24

250 g (9 oz) boneless white fish fillets

2 tablespoons plain (all-purpose) flour

1 egg white

20 g (¾ oz/¼ cup) cornflake crumbs

mayonnaise, to serve

1 Preheat the oven to 180°C (350°F/Gas 4). Cut the fish into pieces about 3 cm (1¼ inches) square. Coat the fish pieces in the flour. Shake off any excess flour.

2 Whisk the egg white in a small bowl. Dip the fish, one piece at a time, in the egg white. Coat with the cornflake crumbs. Place in a single layer on a baking tray.

3 Bake for 15 minutes, or until golden, turning the pieces over after 10 minutes. Serve warm with some mayonnaise.

pirate ship cookies

MAKES ABOUT 8–10

150 g (5½ oz/1 cup) chopped dark chocolate

250 g (9 oz/1 cup) unsalted butter, softened

115 g (4 oz/½ cup) caster (superfine) sugar

310 g (11 oz/2½ cups) plain (all-purpose) flour

pirate ship cookie cutter

icing (frosting)

60 g (2¼ oz/½ cup) icing (confectioners') sugar, sifted

5 g (⅛ oz) butter

1 tablespoon hot water

¼ teaspoon vanilla extract

few drops of red and blue food colouring

1 Preheat the oven to 160°C (315°F/Gas 2–3). Lightly grease two baking trays with butter or oil.

2 Place the chocolate in a heatproof bowl over a saucepan of simmering water, making sure the bowl doesn't touch the water. Stir until melted.

3 Cream the butter and sugar in a bowl using electric beaters until pale and fluffy. Add the melted chocolate. Sift in the flour and stir to make a soft dough.

4 Roll out the dough on a lightly floured surface. Cut out shapes using a pirate ship cookie cutter. Place on the baking trays spaced well apart and flatten slightly.

5 Bake for 12–15 minutes. Allow to cool on the trays for a few minutes, then transfer to a wire rack to cool.

6 To make the icing, blend all the ingredients together until smooth. Separate into bowls, then add the food colouring. Spread over the cookies to decorate.

Note: You can find this cookie cutter in specialty kitchenware stores or try online stores.

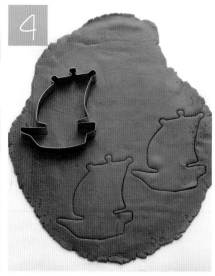

lifesavers

MAKES 5

5 cm (2 inch) round cookie cutter

2 egg whites

115 g (4 oz/½ cup) caster (superfine) sugar

3 tablespoons whipped cream

strawberry or raspberry jam, for spreading

fine ribbon, to decorate

1. Preheat the oven to 150°C (300°F/Gas 2). Line a baking tray with baking paper. Use a 5 cm (2 inch) round cookie cutter to draw 10 circles on the baking paper.

2. Beat the egg whites using electric beaters until stiff peaks form. Add the sugar, a tablespoon at a time, beating well after each tablespoon. Beat until the mixture is thick and glossy, and the sugar has dissolved.

3. Place the mixture in a piping (icing) bag fitted with a plain nozzle. Pipe around the inside edge of the marked circles only.

4. Bake for 20–30 minutes, or until meringues are pale and dry. Turn the oven off. Leave the meringues to cool in the oven with the door slightly open.

5. Near serving time, sandwich two meringues together with jam and cream. As decoration (do not eat!) thread ribbon through the centre and tie a knot or bow.

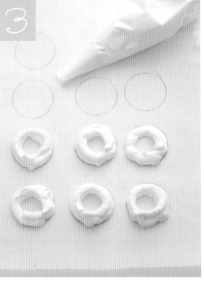

berry iceblocks

MAKES 4–6

300 g (10¹⁄₂ oz) mixed berries
2 tablespoons lemon juice
icing (confectioners') sugar, to taste

1 Blend the berries in a blender until smooth. Push the mixture through a sieve and add the lemon juice. Sweeten to taste with icing sugar.

2 Pour the mixture into four or six plastic iceblock (popsicle) moulds, dropping any extra berries into the mixture. Freeze for 30 minutes.

3 Add iceblock sticks and refreeze for 2¹⁄₂–3 hours, or until the mixture is frozen solid.

ice cream cannonballs

MAKES 24

400 g (14 oz) ice cream (you can use any
flavour you like. We used vanilla)

250 g (9 oz/1²/₃ cups) milk or dark
chocolate melts (buttons)

1 Soften the ice cream slightly and
   spread it out in a shallow container so
   it's 2.5 cm (1 inch) deep. Freeze until
   frozen solid.

2 Cover a baking tray with baking
   paper and place in the freezer. Using
   a melon baller, scoop out tiny balls
   of ice cream and place them on the
   baking tray. Put a cocktail stick in
   each ice cream ball. Cover the tray
   tightly with plastic wrap, making sure
   it is completely covered so the ice
   cream doesn't dry out, then refreeze
   overnight so the balls are frozen solid.

3 Place the chocolate in a heatproof
   bowl over a saucepan of simmering
   water, making sure the bowl doesn't
   touch the water. Stir until the
   chocolate has melted. Remove the
   bowl and set aside to cool a little.

4 Ladle some of the melted chocolate
   into a separate bowl. Work with just
   a few balls at a time so they do not
   melt. Dip each ball in the chocolate
   and place it back on the tray. Return
   to the freezer. Reheat the chocolate if
   necessary. Add more melted chocolate
   to the bowl if needed. Freeze until you
   are ready to serve.

off to
the circus

small toffees

MAKES 24

220 g (7¾ oz/4 cups) sugar

1 tablespoon white vinegar

sprinkles, to decorate

1 Line 24 mini muffin holes with paper patty cases.

2 Combine the sugar, 250 ml (9 fl oz/ 1 cup) water and vinegar in a large, heavy-based saucepan. Stir over medium heat without boiling until the sugar has completely dissolved. Brush the sugar crystals from the sides of the pan with a wet pastry brush. Bring to the boil, then reduce the heat slightly. Boil without stirring for about 20 minutes. Remove from the heat immediately.

3 Pour into the muffin holes and top with sprinkles. Leave to set at room temperature.

Note: Store toffees in an airtight container in a cool dry place for up to 7 days.

iced banana smoothie

SERVES 4

4 bananas

750 ml (26 fl oz/3 cups) milk

4 scoops vanilla ice cream

2 tablespoons honey

ground cinnamon, to dust

1 Combine all the ingredients in a blender. Blend until smooth.

2 Pour into glasses and dust with some cinnamon.

crazy chicken sticks

MAKES ABOUT 32

3 tablespoons teriyaki sauce

1 tablespoon plain yoghurt

2 teaspoons curry powder

4 boneless, skinless chicken breasts,
cut into strips

100 g (3½ oz/2 cups) cornflakes, crushed

40 g (1½ oz/¼ cup) sesame seeds

35 g (1¼ oz) parmesan cheese, grated

sweet and sour sauce

1 tablespoon cornflour (cornstarch)

125 ml (4 fl oz/½ cup) white vinegar

115 g (4 oz/½ cup) caster (superfine) sugar

3 tablespoons tomato sauce (ketchup)

1 teaspoon chicken stock (bouillon) powder

1 Combine the teriyaki sauce, yoghurt and curry powder in a bowl. Add the chicken strips. Mix well, then cover and refrigerate overnight.

2 Preheat the oven to 190°C (375°F/Gas 5). Lightly grease a baking tray with oil.

3 Combine the cornflakes, sesame seeds and parmesan in a shallow dish. Coat each chicken strip in the crumb mixture.

4 Place the strips in a single layer on the baking tray. Bake for 20–25 minutes, or until crisp and golden.

5 To make the sauce, blend the cornflour with the vinegar. Add the remaining ingredients and 250 ml (9 fl oz/1 cup) water in a small saucepan. Stir over medium heat until the mixture boils and thickens. Serve with the chicken strips.

Note: The cooked chicken strips can be frozen in a single layer for up to 2 months.

party sausage rolls

MAKES 36

3 sheets frozen puff pastry, thawed

2 eggs, lightly beaten

750 g (1 lb 10 oz) minced (ground) sausage

1 onion, finely chopped

1 garlic clove, crushed

80 g (2¾ oz/1 cup) fresh breadcrumbs

3 tablespoons chopped flat-leaf (Italian) parsley

3 tablespoons chopped thyme

½ teaspoon ground sage

½ teaspoon freshly grated nutmeg

½ teaspoon ground cloves

½ teaspoon black pepper

1 Preheat the oven to 200°C (400°F/Gas 6). Lightly grease two baking trays.

2 Cut the pastry sheets in half and lightly brush the edges with some of the beaten egg.

3 To make the filling, mix half the remaining egg with the rest of the ingredients in a large bowl. Divide into six even portions.

4 Spoon the filling down the centre of each piece of pastry, then brush the edges with some of the egg.

5 Fold the pastry over the filling, overlapping the edges and placing the join underneath. Brush the rolls with more egg, then cut each into six short pieces. Cut two small slashes on top of each roll.

6 Place on the baking trays and bake for 15 minutes. Reduce the heat to 180°C (350°F/Gas 4) and bake for another 15 minutes, or until puffed and golden.

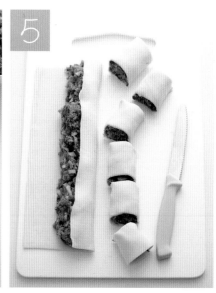

toffee apples

MAKES 12

12 small red or green apples (very crisp)
880 g (1 lb 15 oz/4 cups) sugar
2 tablespoons white vinegar
12 iceblock (popsicle) sticks
red or green food colouring

1 Line two baking trays with foil. Brush with oil.

2 Push a wooden iceblock (popsicle) stick into the stem end of each apple.

3 Combine the sugar, 500 ml (17 fl oz/2 cups) water and vinegar in a heavy-based saucepan. Stir over medium heat without boiling until the sugar has dissolved. Brush the sugar crystals from the sides of the pan with a wet pastry brush. Add the food colouring. Bring to the boil, reduce the heat, then boil without stirring for about 15 minutes. Remove from the heat.

4 Dip the apples, one at a time, into the syrup to coat. Lift out and twist quickly to coat evenly. Drain, then place each apple on the baking tray. Leave to set at room temperature.

rainbow popcorn

MAKES ABOUT 4 CUPS

2 tablespoons oil
½ cup popping corn
330 g (11¾ oz/1½ cups) sugar
50 g (1¾ oz) butter
2–3 drops red food colouring
2–3 drops purple food colouring
2–3 drops yellow food colouring

1 Preheat the oven to 180°C (350°F/Gas 4). Heat the oil in a large frying pan. Add the corn, cover and cook. Hold the lid tightly. Cook until the popping stops.

2 Combine the sugar, butter and 125 ml (4 fl oz/½ cup) water in a heavy-based saucepan. Stir until the sugar has dissolved. Bring to the boil, then boil for 5 minutes.

3 Divide the syrup into three portions and place into bowls. Add the colouring to each bowl and stir. Add the popcorn and toss until the popcorn is coated.

4 Place the popcorn onto a baking tray and bake for 5 minutes. Place the popcorn in a large bowl and toss.

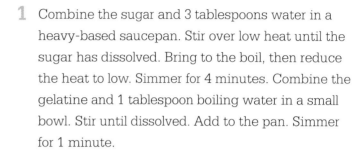

marshmallow cone surprises

MAKES 20

220 g (7¾ oz/1 cup) sugar

3 teaspoons powdered gelatine

3 egg whites

20 small round or square ice cream cones

assorted sweets (candy), for filling

sprinkles, to decorate

1 Combine the sugar and 3 tablespoons water in a heavy-based saucepan. Stir over low heat until the sugar has dissolved. Bring to the boil, then reduce the heat to low. Simmer for 4 minutes. Combine the gelatine and 1 tablespoon boiling water in a small bowl. Stir until dissolved. Add to the pan. Simmer for 1 minute.

2 Beat the egg whites in a bowl until stiff peaks form. Beat in hot syrup and beat for 10–15 minutes.

3 Place the ice cream cones on a baking tray. Fill the bases with sweets. Spoon the mixture into a piping (icing) bag fitted with a fluted nozzle. Pipe swirls of marshmallow into each cone. Spread sprinkles on a piece of baking paper. Dip the cone to coat well. Leave to set overnight.

ice cream sandwiches

MAKES 8

16 small fresh waffles or chocolate chip cookies (use whatever you like)

8 large scoops ice cream (you can use any flavour — we used chocolate but you can try mint choc-chip, rainbow or raspberry swirl for a bit of colour and fun flavours)

sprinkles, to decorate (if you like)

1 Line a 20 x 20 cm (8 x 8 inch) tin or dish with baking paper, leaving an overhang of paper on two opposite sides. Melt the ice cream slightly, then spread into the tin and freeze until firm.

2 Remove the ice cream from the freezer and use the overhanging baking paper to lift from the tin. Cut eight squares or rounds from the ice cream to match the size of your waffles or cookies.

3 To assemble, place eight waffles or cookies on a tray, top each with the ice cream and then the remaining waffles or cookies. Smooth the sides of the ice cream to neaten. Freeze for 5 minutes to firm. Dip the sides in sprinkles to decorate, if you like.

crazy cupcakes

MAKES 12

250 g (9 oz/2 cups) self-raising flour

165 g (5¾ oz/¾ cup) sugar

125 g (4½ oz) unsalted butter, softened

3 eggs

3 tablespoons milk

½ teaspoon vanilla extract

icing (frosting)

125 g (4½ oz) unsalted butter

250 g (9 oz/2 cups) icing (confectioners') sugar

2 tablespoons milk

assorted food colouring

sprinkles, to decorate (if you like)

1 Preheat the oven to 180°C (350°F/Gas 4). Line 12 standard muffin holes with paper patty cases.

2 Sift the flour and sugar into a bowl. Add the butter, eggs, milk and vanilla and beat until smooth. Fill the patty cases three-quarters full with the mixture.

3 Bake for 15 minutes, or until lightly golden. Cool on a wire rack.

4 To make the icing, beat the butter in a small mixing bowl using electric beaters until light and fluffy. Add the sifted icing sugar and milk and beat until smooth.

5 Divide the icing into three or four portions depending on how many colours you want to use. Tint portions of the icing in different colours.

6 Fill a piping (icing) bag fitted with a large star tube with the icing and pipe swirls on the cupcakes. Decorate with sprinkles if you like.

fairy princess tea party

pretty fairy bread

SERVES 8

8 slices white bread
40 g (1½ oz) butter, softened
assorted coloured sprinkles
heart-shaped cookie cutter

1 Spread the bread with butter, then remove the crusts.

2 Place a heart-shaped cookie cutter on the centre of the slice as a guide.

3 Sprinkle a light coating of one type of sprinkle inside the cookie cutter. Sprinkle another type of sprinkle outside the cutter.

4 Remove the cookie cutter. Press in the sprinkles gently using your fingers.

foaming fairy potion

MAKES 1

100 ml (3½ fl oz) creaming soda

1 small scoop vanilla ice cream

sprinkles or pink sugar, to decorate (if you like)

1 Pour the creaming soda into a tall glasses.

2 Add the ice cream and stir gently to make the drink foamy. (Don't stir too hard or the drink will 'boil over'.)

3 Sprinkle with pink sugar and serve immediately.

coconut ice

MAKES 30 PIECES

310 g (11 oz/2½ cups) icing (confectioners') sugar

¼ teaspoon cream of tartar

1 egg white, lightly beaten

3 tablespoons condensed milk

155 g (5½ oz/1¾ cups) desiccated coconut

pink food colouring

1 Lightly grease a 26 x 8 x 4.5 cm (10½ x 3¼ x 1¾ inch) loaf (bar) tin with oil. Line the base with baking paper and grease the paper.

2 Sift the icing sugar and cream of tartar into a bowl. Make a well in the centre. Add the egg white and condensed milk. Using a wooden spoon, stir in half the coconut. Add the rest of the coconut. Mix until well combined.

3 Put two-thirds of the mixture in a bowl. Add the pink colouring and knead the colour through.

4 Press half the pink mixture into the loaf tin. Cover with the white mixture and press down gently. Add the remaining pink mixture and press down gently. Refrigerate for 1 hour, or until set. When firm, remove from the tin and cut into squares or rectangles.

Note: Coconut ice can be stored in an airtight container in a cool, dark place for up to 2 weeks.

white chocolate mousse

SERVES 8

100 g (3½ oz) white chocolate melts

125 ml (4 fl oz/½ cup) skim milk

2 teaspoons powdered gelatine

400 g (14 oz) low-fat French vanilla fromage frais or whipped yoghurt

3 egg whites

3 tablespoons passionfruit pulp

icing (confectioners') sugar, to dust

1. Place the chocolate and milk in a small saucepan and stir over low heat until the chocolate has melted. Leave to cool.

2. Place 3 tablespoons boiling water in a heatproof bowl. Sprinkle evenly with the gelatine and stir until dissolved. Using a wooden spoon, stir the gelatine into the chocolate mixture.

3. Place the fromage frais in a large bowl and gradually stir in the chocolate mixture, a little at a time, stirring until smooth.

4. Beat the egg whites in a clean, dry bowl using electric beaters until soft peaks form. Gently fold the egg whites and the passionfruit pulp into the chocolate mixture.

5. Divide the mixture among eight 125 ml (4 fl oz/½ cup) cups or ramekins. Refrigerate for 3 hours, or until set. Serve with a light dusting of icing sugar.

fairy cakes

MAKES 12

120 g (4¼ oz) unsalted butter, softened

145 g (5½ oz/⅔ cup) caster (superfine) sugar

185 g (6½ oz/1½ cups) self-raising flour

125 ml (4 fl oz/½ cup) milk

2 teaspoons vanilla extract

2 eggs

125 ml (4 fl oz/½ cup) pouring (whipping) cream

105 g (3¾ oz/⅓ cup) strawberry jam

icing (confectioners') sugar, to dust

1 Preheat the oven to 180°C (350°F/Gas 4). Line 12 standard muffin holes with paper patty cases.

2 Beat the butter, sugar, flour, milk, vanilla and eggs in a bowl using electric beaters on low speed for about 2 minutes. Increase the speed and beat for 2 minutes, or until smooth and pale.

3 Divide the mixture evenly among the cases. Bake for 20 minutes, or until lightly golden. Transfer to a wire rack to cool.

4 Whip the cream using electric beaters until soft peaks form.

5 Using a small sharp knife, cut shallow rounds from the top of each cake. Cut these in half. Spoon 2 teaspoons of the cream into the hole in each cake. Spread 1 teaspoon of the jam in the centre.

6 Position the two halves of the cake tops in the jam so they look like butterfly wings. Dust the cakes with icing sugar.

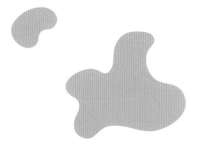

fluffy coconut cupcakes

MAKES 36

250 g (9 oz/2 cups) self-raising flour, sifted

45 g (1²/₃ oz/½ cup) desiccated coconut

230 g (8½ oz/1 cup) caster (superfine) sugar

250 ml (9 fl oz/1 cup) buttermilk

2 eggs, lightly beaten

1 teaspoon natural coconut extract

125 g (4½ oz) unsalted butter, melted

coconut icing (frosting)

280 g (10 oz/2¼ cups) icing
(confectioners') sugar

135 g (4¾ oz/1½ cups) desiccated coconut

75 g (2½ oz) unsalted butter, softened

½ teaspoon natural coconut extract

2 tablespoons hot water

pink sugar crystals,
to sprinkle

1   Preheat the oven to 180°C (350°F/Gas 4). Line 36 standard muffin holes with paper patty cases.

2   Combine the flour, coconut and sugar in a bowl and make a well in the centre.

3   Combine the buttermilk, eggs, coconut extract and butter in a bowl. Add to the flour mixture and mix until combined.

4   Divide the mixture evenly among the cases. Bake for 12 minutes, or until a skewer comes out clean when inserted into the centre of a cake. Transfer onto a wire rack to cool.

5   To make the coconut icing, combine the icing sugar and coconut in a bowl. Add the butter, coconut extract and enough hot water to make an icing that will be easy to spread.

6   Decorate each cake with a thick covering of icing and sprinkle with pink sugar crystals.

sparkly fairy wands

MAKES 10

90 g (3¼ oz) butter, chopped

80 g (2¾ oz/⅓ cup) caster (superfine) sugar

90 g (3¼ oz/¾ cup) plain (all-purpose) flour

30 g (1 oz/¼ cup) self-raising flour

2 tablespoons custard powder (instant vanilla pudding mix)

1 egg, lightly beaten

200 g (7 oz) white chocolate melts, melted

10 iceblock (popsicle) sticks

star-shaped cookie cutter

icing (frosting), to decorate (see page 17)

coloured silver balls (cachous), coloured sugar or pink sprinkles

1 Place the butter, sugar, flours and custard powder in a food processor. Process for 30 seconds or until fine and crumbly. Add the egg and process for 20 seconds, or until a soft dough forms.

2 Turn onto a floured surface and knead for 30 seconds. Cover with plastic wrap and refrigerate for 1 hour.

3 Preheat the oven to 180°C (350°F/Gas 4). Line two baking trays with baking paper. Roll the dough out between two sheets of baking paper to a 3 mm (⅛ inch) thickness. Cut the dough into star shapes using a 9 cm (3½ inch) star-shaped cutter.

4 Arrange the stars on the baking trays and bake for 15 minutes or until golden. Cool on the trays.

5 Place ½ teaspoon of melted chocolate on the flat side of half of the biscuits. Attach the sticks. Sandwich the remaining biscuits over the chocolate and press to secure. Allow the chocolate to set.

6 To decorate, put small dots of icing on one side of the biscuit. Top with coloured balls. Leave to set.

into the wild

dinosaur cookies

MAKES ABOUT 32

125 g (4½ oz) unsalted butter, softened

115 g (4 oz) caster (superfine) sugar

1 egg, lightly beaten

½ teaspoon natural vanilla extract

225 g (8 oz) plain (all-purpose) flour

30 g (1 oz/¼ cup) cocoa powder

½ teaspoon baking powder

2 teaspoons ground cinnamon

1 egg white

1 tablespoon caster (superfine) sugar, extra

1 teaspoon ground cinnamon, extra

dinosaur-shaped cookie cutters

icing (frosting), to decorate (see page 17)

1 Preheat the oven to 190°C (375°F/ Gas 5). Grease two baking trays.

2 Cream the butter and sugar in a bowl using electric beaters. Beat in the egg and vanilla. Sift in the flour, cocoa powder, baking powder and cinnamon and stir into the mixture until a dough forms. Cover the dough with plastic wrap and refrigerate for 30 minutes.

3 Roll out the dough between two sheets of baking paper to 5 mm (¼ inch) thick. Cut out using dinosaur cookie cutters. Place on the trays.

4 Whisk the egg white. Combine the extra sugar and cinnamon in a bowl.

5 Brush the tops of the biscuits with the glaze, scatter over the cinnamon sugar and bake for 10 minutes. Decorate with icing if you like.

green punch

SERVES 2–3

1 green apple, cored

½ medium honeydew melon, peeled, seeds removed

2 oranges, peeled

ice cubes, to serve

1 Cut the apple, melon and oranges into pieces to fit into a fruit juicer.

2 Using the plunger, push all the ingredients through the juicer and into a pitcher.

3 Pour into glasses and serve with ice.

chicken drumsticks with ranch dressing

MAKES 32

32 small chicken drumsticks

1 tablespoon garlic salt

1 tablespoon onion powder

oil, for deep-frying

250 ml (9 fl oz/1 cup) tomato sauce (ketchup)

4 tablespoons Worcestershire sauce

40 g (1½ oz) butter, melted

1 tablespoon sugar

Tabasco sauce, to taste

Ranch dressing

250 g (9 oz/1 cup) mayonnaise

250 g (9 oz/1 cup) sour cream

4 tablespoons lemon juice

20 g (¾ oz) snipped chives

1 Remove the skin from the chicken and use a large knife to cut off the knuckle. Wash the chicken thoroughly and pat dry with paper towel.

2 Combine 1 tablespoon freshly ground black pepper, the garlic salt and onion powder and rub some into each chicken drumstick.

3 Fill a deep heavy-based frying pan or deep-fryer one-third full of oil and heat to 180°C (350°F), or until a cube of bread dropped into the oil turns golden brown in 15 seconds. Cook the chicken in batches for 2 minutes each batch, then remove with tongs or a slotted spoon and drain on paper towel.

4 Transfer the chicken to a large non-metallic bowl or shallow dish. Combine the tomato sauce, Worcestershire sauce, butter, sugar and Tabasco sauce, pour over the chicken and stir to coat. Refrigerate the chicken, covered, for several hours, or overnight.

5 Heat the barbecue hotplate before cooking so it is very hot and grease with a little oil. Cook the chicken for 20–25 minutes, or until cooked through. Turn and brush with the marinade during cooking.

6 To make the dressing, combine the mayonnaise, sour cream, lemon juice and chives and season to taste. Serve the chicken with the ranch dressing.

beef and bean burritos

MAKES 8

2 tablespoons oil

1 onion, sliced

1 tablespoon ground cumin

2 teaspoons ground coriander

½ teaspoon ground cinnamon

1 teaspoon chilli powder

600 g (1 lb 5 oz) minced (ground) beef

425 g (15 oz) tomatoes, chopped

4 tablespoons tomato paste
(concentrated purée)

440 g (15½ oz) tinned kidney beans, drained

270 g (9½ oz) tinned corn kernels, drained

8 flour tortillas

Topping

160 g (5¾ oz) cheddar cheese, grated

3 tablespoons taco sauce (if you like)

1 Heat the oil in a large heavy-based frying pan. Add the onion, spices and beef. Cook over medium–high heat for 10 minutes until well browned and almost all the liquid has evaporated. Use a fork to break up any lumps of the minced beef as it cooks. Reduce the heat to low and add the tomatoes and paste. Cover and cook, stirring occasionally, for 20 minutes. Add the kidney beans and corn and stir until heated through.

2 Preheat the oven to 180°C (350°F/Gas 4). To assemble the burritos, place about ½ cup of minced beef mixture on each tortilla. Roll the tortillas around the filling and place, seam-side down, on a baking tray.

3 Sprinkle the burritos with the grated cheese. Bake for 10 minutes, or until the cheese has melted. Top each burrito with taco sauce, if you like, and serve immediately.

jungle burgers

MAKES 10

500 g (1 lb 2 oz) minced (ground) beef

1 small onion, finely chopped

1 tablespoon finely chopped parsley

1 egg, lightly beaten

1 tablespoon tomato sauce (ketchup)

½ teaspoon herb pepper

2 tablespoons oil

10 small dinner rolls, cut in half

2 large handfuls finely shredded lettuce

2 small tomatoes, thinly sliced

5 rings tinned pineapple, drained and halved

5 cheese slices, halved

barbecue or tomato sauce (ketchup), to serve

1 Combine the beef, onion, parsley, beaten egg, tomato sauce and herb pepper in a large bowl. Using your hands, mix until well combined. Divide the mixture into 10 portions. Shape into round patties.

2 Heat the oil in a large, heavy-based frying pan over medium heat. Cook the patties for 5 minutes on each side, or until they are well browned. Remove and drain on paper towel.

3 To assemble the burgers, place a patty on the base of a roll. Top with the lettuce, tomato, pineapple slice and cheese slice. Add some sauce and finish with a roll top. Serve immediately.

cavemen clubs

MAKES 9

3 large bananas, peeled and cut into 3 pieces

9 wooden iceblock (popsicle) sticks

125 g (4½ oz) dark chocolate, chopped

20 g (¾ oz) white vegetable shortening (Copha)

80 g (2¾ oz/½ cup) crushed nuts (you can also use sprinkles or crushed sweets)

1 Line a baking tray with foil. Carefully push an iceblock stick into each piece of banana. Place on the tray and freeze for 2 hours, or until firm.

2 Combine the chocolate and shortening in a small heatproof bowl. Stand the bowl over a saucepan of simmering water and stir until the chocolate has melted and the mixture is smooth.

3 Working one at a time, dip each banana piece into the hot chocolate mixture and drain off any excess chocolate. Roll half of each chocolate-coated banana in the crushed nuts. Place on the tray. Refrigerate until the chocolate has set, then wrap in plastic wrap and place in the freezer for at least 2 hours.

swamp mud

SERVES 8

150 g (5½ oz) dark cooking chocolate, chopped

4 eggs, separated

2 tablespoons caster (superfine) sugar

1 teaspoon grated orange zest

4 tablespoons whipping cream

1 teaspoon powdered gelatine

1 tablespoon orange juice

sprinkles, for decoration

1 Place the chocolate in a small heatproof bowl. Stand the bowl over a saucepan of simmering water. Stir until the chocolate has melted and the mixture is smooth. Leave to cool slightly.

2 Beat the egg yolks, sugar and zest in a large bowl using electric beaters for 5 minutes or until thick and creamy. Beat in the cream and melted chocolate.

3 Combine the gelatine and juice in a small bowl. Stand the bowl in hot water. Stir until the gelatine dissolves. Add to the chocolate mixture and beat until combined.

4 Place the egg whites in a bowl. Using electric beaters, beat until firm peaks form. Add to the chocolate mixture. Fold until well combined. Refrigerate for 2 hours, or until set. Top with sprinkles to decorate.

mini mud cakes

MAKES 30

185 g (6½ oz/¾ cup) caster (superfine) sugar

175 g (6 oz) dark chocolate, chopped

90 g (3¼ oz) unsalted butter, chopped

2 eggs, lightly beaten

60 g (2¼ oz/½ cup) plain (all-purpose) flour

60 g (2¼ oz/½ cup) self-raising flour

30 g (1 oz/¼ cup) unsweetened cocoa powder

200 g (7 oz) milk chocolate melts, chopped

125 ml (4 fl oz/½ cup) cream

1 Preheat the oven to 180°C (350°F/Gas 4). Lightly grease a 20 x 30 cm (8 x 12 inch) baking tin. Cover the base and two long sides with baking paper.

2 Place the sugar, chocolate, butter and 3 tablespoons water in a saucepan. Stir over low heat for 5 minutes, or until melted. Remove from the heat and leave to cool to room temperature. Stir in the eggs and 2 tablespoons water.

3 Sift the flours and cocoa into a bowl and make a well in the centre. Pour the chocolate mixture into the well. Mix well and pour into the baking tin.

4 Bake for 20–25 minutes. Cool in the tin for 5 minutes, then remove and cool on a wire rack.

5 Cut cake into squares or cut 30 rounds using a 3 cm (1¼ inch) round cutter. Place the cakes, top side down, on a wire cake rack over a baking tray.

6 Place the chocolate melts in a bowl. Heat the cream until hot and pour over the chocolate. Leave for 2 minutes, then stir until the melted. Spoon the mixture over the cakes. Reheat the chocolate if it becomes too thick.

dinosaur eggs

MAKES 40

180 g (6½ oz/1 cup) dried apricots, finely chopped

90 g (3¼ oz/1 cup) desiccated coconut

125 ml (4 fl oz/½ cup) sweetened condensed milk

desiccated coconut, extra

1 Combine the apricots, coconut and condensed milk in a bowl and mix well.

2 Roll 2 teaspoons of the mixture into a small ball. Repeat with the remaining mixture. Roll the balls in the extra desiccated coconut. Refrigerate until set.

teddy bears' picnic

mini marble cakes

SERVES 6

1 teaspoon natural vanilla extract

185 g (6½ oz) unsalted butter, chopped

230 g (8 oz/1 cup) caster (superfine) sugar

3 eggs

280 g (10 oz/2¼ cups) self-raising flour

185 ml (6 fl oz/¾ cup) milk

2 tablespoons unsweetened cocoa powder

1½ tablespoons warm milk, extra

1 Preheat the oven to 200°C (400°F/ Gas 6). Lightly grease eight mini loaf (bar) tins and line the bases with baking paper.

2 Combine the vanilla extract, butter and sugar in a bowl and beat using electric beaters until fluffy. Add the eggs one at a time, beating well after each addition. Sift the flour, then fold it into the creamed mixture with the milk. Divide the mixture in half and put the second half into a clean bowl.

3 Combine the cocoa powder and warm milk in a bowl and stir until smooth, then add to one half of the cake mixture, stirring. Spoon the two mixtures into the tin in alternate spoonfuls. Using a skewer, cut through the mixture four times to create a marble effect.

4 Bake for 50–60 minutes. Leave in the tin for 5 minutes, then turn out onto a wire rack to cool.

caramel milkshake

SERVES 2

250 ml (9 fl oz/1 cup) cold milk

2 scoops vanilla ice cream

3 tablespoons caramel fudge sauce

1 Blend the milk, ice cream and caramel fudge sauce in a blender until smooth.

2 Pour into glasses and serve immediately.

caramel scrolls

MAKES 16

310 g (11 oz/2½ cups) self-raising flour

115 g (4 oz/½ cup) caster (superfine) sugar

125 g (4½ oz) butter

125 ml (4 fl oz/½ cup) milk

3 tablespoons sour cream

60 g (2¼ oz) butter, extra, softened

60 g (2¼ oz/⅓ cup) soft brown sugar

caramel icing (frosting)

45 g (1½ oz) butter

45 g (1½ oz/¼ cup) soft brown sugar

1 tablespoon milk

60 g (2¼ oz/½ cup) icing (confectioners') sugar, sifted

1. Preheat the oven to 210°C (415°F/Gas 6–7). Brush a shallow 23 cm (9 inch) square cake tin with oil.

2. Sift the flour into a bowl. Add the caster sugar and butter. Rub the butter into the flour until crumbly.

3. Add the combined milk and sour cream to the bowl. Stir until the mixture is almost smooth.

4. Turn the dough onto a floured surface. Knead until smooth. Roll out the dough on a floured surface to a large rectangle.

5. Combine the extra butter and brown sugar in a bowl. Spread the mixture evenly over the dough.

6. Roll dough from the long side into a log. Cut into 16 pieces. Place the slices, flat side down, in the tin.

7. Bake for 25 minutes, or until lightly golden.

8. To make the icing, melt the butter in a saucepan. Add the brown sugar and milk. Stir over low heat for 1 minute. Add the icing sugar and stir until smooth. Spread the cakes with the icing.

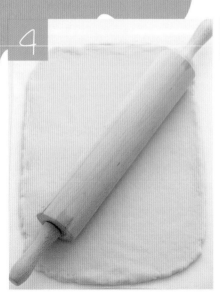
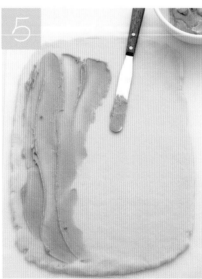
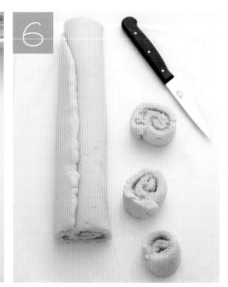

fruity dip

125 g (4½ oz/½ cup) vanilla-flavoured yoghurt

assorted fruit, such as banana, pear, apple, kiwi fruit, pawpaw, watermelon, strawberries or whatever is in season

1 Pour the flavoured yoghurt into a serving dish.

2 Grate or cut the fruit into small pieces. Serve with the yoghurt for dipping.

chocolate strawberries

SERVES 8–10

250 g (9 oz) strawberries
150 g (5½ oz) milk chocolate
100 g (3½ oz) white chocolate

1 Brush the strawberries with a dry pastry brush to remove any dirt.

2 Melt the dark chocolate in a small heatproof bowl set over a saucepan of steaming water, making sure the base of the bowl does not touch the water. Dip the bottom half of each strawberry in the chocolate. Put on a baking tray lined with baking paper and allow to set.

3 When set, melt the white chocolate in the same way as the dark. Dip the tips of the strawberries in the chocolate and allow to set on the baking tray. Refrigerate until ready to serve.

petit croque-monsieur

MAKES 24

16 slices white bread

125 g (4½ oz/½ cup) wholegrain mustard

100 g (3½ oz) thinly shaved honey ham

100 g (3½ oz) Jarlsberg cheese, thinly sliced

40 g (1½ oz) butter

2 tablespoons olive oil

1 Spread each slice of bread with mustard. Lay out eight bread slices on a board, mustard-side-up. Top with the shaved ham, then the cheese slices.

2 Press the remaining bread slices on top, mustard side down, to make eight sandwiches. Trim off the crusts, then cut each sandwich into three fingers.

3 Melt half the butter and oil in a non-stick frying pan. When the butter begins to foam, cook half the fingers until crisp and golden on both sides and the cheese is just starting to melt. Remove and keep warm on a baking tray in the oven. Melt the remaining butter and oil in the frying pan and cook the remaining fingers. Serve warm.

chocolate-chip ice cream sandwich

MAKES 4–6

300 g (10½ oz) frozen chocolate pound cake

1 litre (35 fl oz/4 cups) chocolate chip
ice cream, softened

1 Using a sharp knife, cut the pound cake horizontally into four thin slices. Using a 6.5 cm (2½ inch) plain cutter, cut eight rounds from the slices of cake. You will need two rounds of cake per person.

2 Line a 20 x 20 cm (8 x 8 inch) tin or dish with baking paper, leaving an overhang of paper on two opposite sides.

3 Soften the ice cream and pour into the tin. Freeze for 2 hours, or until firm. Remove the ice cream from the freezer and use the overhanging baking paper to lift out.

4 Using a 6.5 cm (2½ inch) round cutter, cut four rounds from the ice cream.

5 To assemble, place four slices of cake on a tray, top each with a round of ice cream and then the remaining slices of cake. Smooth the sides of the ice cream to neaten, if necessary. Return the sandwiches to the freezer for 5 minutes to firm.

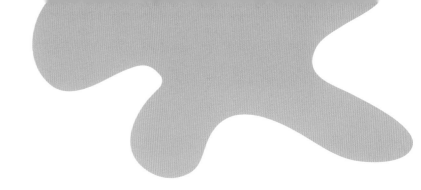

frozen banana bites

MAKES 18

3 large bananas, peeled and cut into 6 pieces

9 wooden iceblock (popsicle) sticks

100 g (3½ oz) dark chocolate, chopped

20 g (¾ oz) white vegetable shortening (Copha)

1 Line a large baking tray with foil. Cut the iceblock sticks in half. Carefully push a stick into each piece of banana.

2 Combine the chocolate and shortening in a small heatproof bowl. Set over a saucepan of simmering water. Stir until melted and the mixture is smooth.

3 Working one at a time, dip each banana piece into the hot chocolate mixture. Drain off any excess chocolate. Place onto the tray. Refrigerate until the chocolate is set. Freeze for at least 2 hours.

Note: Frozen banana bites should be eaten on the day they are made.

choc-dipped ice cream balls

MAKES 36

500 g (1 lb 2 oz) ice cream (we used chocolate but you can use any flavour you like)

450 g (1 lb) milk chocolate

30 g (1 oz/½ cup) shredded coconut, toasted

1 Line two large baking trays with baking paper and place in the freezer to chill. Use a melon baller to make 36 balls of ice cream and place on the baking trays. Place a cocktail stick in each ice cream ball. Return to the freezer for 1 hour to freeze.

2 Place the chocolate in a heatproof bowl set over a saucepan of steaming water, making sure the base of the bowl does not touch the water. Stir occasionally until the chocolate has melted. Remove the bowl from the heat and set aside to cool.

3 Put the coconut in a separate small bowl. Dip the balls in the milk chocolate, then the toasted coconut. Freeze the ice cream balls for 1 hour.

disco

ham and cheese balls

MAKES ABOUT 24

80 g (2¾ oz/½ cup) sesame seeds

100 g (3½ oz) soft cream cheese

100 g (3½ oz) ham, finely chopped

50 g (1¾ oz) cheddar cheese, grated

1 Spread the sesame seeds on a baking tray. Toast under a hot grill (broiler) for a few seconds or until golden. Pour onto a plate to cool.

2 Place the cream cheese into a bowl and mash with a fork. Add the ham and cheese and mix to combine.

3 Using your hands, roll teaspoons of the mixture into balls. Roll the balls in the sesame seeds. Refrigerate for 1 hour before serving.

pineapple delight

SERVES 4–6

750 g (1 lb 10 oz) pineapple

500 ml (17 fl oz/2 cups) lemonade

2 tablespoons lime juice

1 Peel the pineapple and remove the centre core. Cut the flesh into 2 cm (3/4 inch) pieces. Blend in a blender for 1–2 minutes, or until as smooth as possible.

2 Pour the lemonade into a pitcher and add the pineapple purée, stirring gently to combine.

3 Add 2 tablespoons of lime juice and mix well. Pour into the serving glasses and serve.

American hot dogs

SERVES 10

10 frankfurts

10 long hot dog rolls

American-style mustard and tomato sauce (ketchup), to serve

1 Cook the frankfurts in a saucepan of simmering water for 5–10 minutes.

2 Split the rolls lengthways. Remove the frankfurts from the water. Place in the roll. Top with the mustard and sauce and serve immediately.

Variations: Hot bean dogs: Make as above, leaving out the mustard. Top with warmed baked beans and grated cheddar cheese.

Hot dog boats: Make as above, leaving out the mustard. Cut 5 cheddar cheese slices in half diagonally. Thread half a wooden skewer through 2 corners. Skewer into the hot dog.

pizza margherita

SERVES 4

4 mini pizza bases

topping

1 tablespoon olive oil

425 g (15 oz) tinned crushed tomatoes

1 bay leaf

1 teaspoon chopped thyme

6 chopped basil leaves

150 g (5½ oz) bocconcini cheese (fresh baby mozzarella cheese), thinly sliced

olive oil, extra, to drizzle

1 Preheat the oven to 210°C (415°F/Gas 6–7).

2 To make the topping, heat the oil in a saucepan over medium heat. Add the tomatoes, bay leaf, thyme and basil and simmer, stirring occasionally, for about 20–25 minutes, or until thick. Leave to cool, then remove the bay leaf.

3 Lightly grease two baking trays. Sprinkle the trays with flour and place the bases on top.

4 Spread the sauce over the pizza bases, leaving a 3 cm (1¼ inch) border.

5 Arrange the bocconcini over the top and drizzle with olive oil. Bake for 15 minutes, or until crisp and bubbling. Serve warm.

chocolate ice cream sundaes

SERVES 6

chocolate fudge sauce

100 g (3½ oz/⅔ cup) dark chocolate, chopped

185 ml (6 fl oz/¾ cup) sweetened condensed milk

4 tablespoons milk

40 g (1½ oz) unsalted butter, diced

1 litre (35 oz/4 cups) vanilla ice cream

6 glacé cherries

12 wafers

sprinkles, to decorate (if you like)

1 To make the chocolate fudge sauce, put the chocolate, condensed milk and milk in a heatproof bowl and set over a saucepan of steaming water, making sure the base of the bowl does not touch the water. Stir occasionally until the chocolate has almost melted. Remove from the heat and stir until smooth.

2 Beat in the butter until melted and smooth. Set aside to cool for about 20 minutes, stirring regularly.

3 To assemble, put two scoops of ice cream into each sundae (parfait) dish.

4 Pour the chocolate fudge sauce over the ice cream. Top each sundae with a glacé cherry and 2 wafers and serve immediately.

melon ball skewers

MAKES ABOUT 15

½ rockmelon or any orange-fleshed melon

½ honeydew melon

¼ watermelon

15 bamboo skewers

1 Remove the seeds from each of the melons. Using a melon baller, scoop the flesh of each melon into balls. Place the balls in a large bowl. Cover and chill well.

2 To serve, skewer one ball of each type of melon onto a bamboo skewer. Repeat until all the fruit is used.

mango and raspberry iceblocks

MAKES 4–6

2 large mangoes

3 tablespoons orange juice

16–24 raspberries

1 Peel the mangoes and purée in a blender or food processor until smooth.

2 Add the orange juice and mix well. Pour into four or six plastic iceblock (popsicle) moulds.

3 Add 4 raspberries into each mould as you fill them. Freeze for 30 minutes.

4 Add the iceblock sticks and freeze for a further 2½–3 hours, or until frozen solid.

Note: Although these iceblocks will keep for 3 weeks, they taste best when eaten on the same day that they are made.

fruity yoghurt pops

MAKES 6

400 g (14 oz) vanilla-flavoured yoghurt

170 g (6 oz) tinned passionfruit pulp in syrup

4 large strawberries, chopped

1 tablespoon icing (confectioners') sugar

2 tablespoons melted chocolate

6 wooden iceblock (popsicle) sticks

1 Combine the yoghurt and passionfruit in a bowl. Add the strawberries and icing sugar. Mix well.

2 Spoon the mixture into six ice cream moulds or paper cups. Freeze for 1 hour.

3 Press a wooden iceblock stick in the centre of each mould. Freeze for 2 hours.

4 Turn the pops out of the moulds. Drizzle with melted chocolate before serving.

popcorn pops

MAKES 6

1 tablespoon oil

¼ cup popping corn

165 g (5¾ oz/¾ cup) sugar

25 g (1 oz) butter

4 drops red or green food colouring

6 wooden iceblock (popsicle) sticks

1 Heat the oil in a large saucepan. Add the corn, cover and cook over medium heat. Hold the lid tightly, shaking the pan occasionally. Cook until the popping stops. Put the popcorn in a large bowl and set aside.

2 Combine the sugar, butter and 3 tablespoons water in a small heavy-based saucepan. Stir over medium heat without boiling until the sugar has completely dissolved. Brush the sugar crystals from the side of the pan with a wet pastry brush. Bring to the boil. Boil without stirring for 5 minutes. Remove from the heat and stir in the food colouring.

3 Pour the syrup over the popcorn. Using two metal spoons, combine well. Allow the mixture to cool until cool enough to handle. With oiled hands and working quickly, press the popcorn firmly into ball shapes around the top of each iceblock stick. Serve on the day of making.

farm party

animal feed

SERVES 10

1 cup plain or assorted rice crackers

1 cup banana crisps

60 g (2¼ oz/1 cup) shredded or
flaked coconut

125 g (4½ oz/1 cup) sultanas
(golden raisins)

125 g (4½ oz/1 cup) raisins

2 cups toasted muesli

4 cups fresh popcorn

125 g (4½ oz/1 cup) sunflower kernels,
pumpkin seeds or pepitas (peeled
pumkin seeds)

1 Combine all the ingredients in a large
bowl and mix well.

2 Spoon into individual bags as a take-
home treat or place in containers
for serving.

home-made lemonade

SERVES 6–8

685 ml (23½ fl oz/2¾ cups) lemon juice

310 g (11 oz/1¼ cups) sugar

ice cubes, to serve

mint leaves, to garnish

1 Combine the lemon juice and sugar in a large bowl and stir until the sugar has dissolved. Pour into a large pitcher.

2 Add 1.25 litres (44 fl oz/5 cups) water to the pitcher and stir well to combine. Refrigerate.

3 To serve, pour over ice cubes and garnish with mint leaves.

corn cobs with butter

SERVES 10

5 corn cobs
125 g (4½ oz) butter

1 Cut the corn cobs in half. Place the corn in a large saucepan of cold water. Bring to the boil and cook for 8–10 minutes, or until the corn is tender.

2 Drain the corn. Place 1–2 teaspoons butter on each piece. Season with salt and pepper.

cheese swags

MAKES 12

6 wholemeal bread slices
6 cheese sticks
6 luncheon meat slices
12 chives

1 Remove the crusts from the bread and flatten with a rolling pin. Place a slice of luncheon meat on each piece of bread, then a cheese stick. Roll up the bread tightly.

2 Tie a chive tightly around both ends of the roll. Cut the rolls in half so that the chive tie is in the centre of each 'swag'.

chicken sausage rolls

MAKES 36

3 frozen puff pastry sheets, thawed

2 eggs, lightly beaten

750 g (1 lb 10 oz) minced (ground) chicken

4 spring onions (scallions), finely chopped

80 g (2¾ oz/1 cup) fresh breadcrumbs

1 carrot, finely grated

2 tablespoons fruit chutney

1 tablespoon sweet chilli sauce

1 tablespoon grated fresh ginger

sesame seeds, to sprinkle

1 Preheat the oven to 200°C (400°F/Gas 6). Lightly grease two baking trays.

2 Cut the pastry sheets in half and lightly brush the edges with some of the beaten egg.

3 Mix half the remaining egg with the remaining ingredients, except the sesame seeds, in a large bowl, then divide into six even portions.

4 Pipe or spoon the filling down the centre of each piece of pastry, then brush the edges with some of the egg.

5 Fold the pastry over the filling, overlapping the edges and placing the join underneath.

6 Brush the rolls with more egg. Sprinkle with sesame seeds, then cut each into six short pieces. Cut two small slashes on top of each roll

7 Place on the baking trays and bake for 15 minutes. Reduce the heat to 180°C (350°F/Gas 4) and bake for another 15 minutes, or until puffed and golden.

sausage sizzle

SERVES 10

1.5 kg (3 lb 5 oz) thick sausages

2 teaspoons oil

60 g (2¼ oz) butter, melted

6 onions, finely sliced

10 long bread rolls, buttered

grated cheese, to serve

shredded lettuce, sliced tomato, and shredded carrot, to serve

coleslaw, to serve

1 Bring a large saucepan of water to the boil. Add the sausages, reduce the heat and cook for 5 minutes. Drain and cool. Pierce the sausages with a fork.

2 Heat the oil and butter in large frying pan. Cook the onion until transparent. Move the onions to one side of the pan. Add the sausages and cook for 10–15 minutes or until sausages have browned and the onions are soft.

3 Fill the rolls with sausage, onion, cheese and salad. Serve the coleslaw in a separate bowl.

chicken burritos

MAKES 8

8 flour tortillas

1 barbecued chicken

325 g (11½ oz) jar mild salsa

2 large tomatoes, sliced

135 g (4¾ oz) shredded lettuce

1 Lebanese (short) cucumber, sliced

250 g (9 oz/2 cups) grated cheddar cheese

1 Preheat the oven to 180°C (350°F/Gas 4). Wrap the flour tortillas in foil and place on a baking tray. Warm in the oven for about 10 minutes.

2 Skin, bone and shred the barbecued chicken. Place the shredded chicken in a frying pan with the salsa and stir together until heated through.

3 Arrange some of the shredded chicken and the sauce in the middle of each of the warm tortillas.

4 Pile the tomato, lettuce, cucumber and cheese on top of the chicken. Roll up and serve.

chocolate haystacks

MAKES 40

440 g (15½ oz/2 cups) sugar

40 g (1½ oz/⅓ cup) unsweetened cocoa powder

125 ml (4 fl oz/½ cup) milk

125 g (4½ oz) butter, chopped

300 g (10½ oz/3 cups) rolled (porridge) oats

90 g (3¼ oz/1½ cups) shredded coconut

1 Combine the sugar and cocoa in a large heavy-based saucepan. Add the milk and butter. Stir over low heat, without boiling, until the butter has melted and the sugar has completely dissolved. Bring the mixture to the boil, stirring constantly. Remove from the heat immediately.

2 Add the rolled oats and shredded coconut. Stir until well combined.

3 Working quickly, drop heaped teaspoons of the chocolate mixture onto baking paper. Allow to set.

Hint: For easier handling, spoon the hot chocolate mixture into paper patty cases.

Note: Store in an airtight container in a cool, dry place until ready to use.

ballerina
party

vanilla sugar hearts

MAKES 36

185 g (6½ oz/¾ cup) unsalted butter, softened

230 g (8½ oz/1 cup) caster (superfine) sugar

2 teaspoons natural vanilla extract

1 egg

310 g (11 oz/2½ cups) plain (all-purpose) flour

75 g (2⅔ oz/⅓ cup) white sugar

1 Cream the butter, caster sugar and vanilla in a bowl using electric beaters until pale and fluffy. Add the egg, beating until just combined. Sift in the flour and stir to form a soft dough.

2 Divide the mixture in two, shape the halves into discs, cover with plastic wrap and refrigerate for 1 hour.

3 Preheat the oven to 180°C (350°F/ Gas 4). Line two baking trays with baking paper.

4 Roll the dough out between two pieces of baking paper to 5 mm (¼ inch) thick. Cut the dough into heart shapes using a 5.5 cm (2¼ inch) heart-shaped cookie cutter.

5 Place on the prepared trays spaced well apart. Sprinkle with the white sugar and gently press into the dough.

6 Bake for 8–10 minutes, or until golden. Allow to cool on the trays for a few minutes, then transfer to a wire rack to cool completely.

strawberry shake

SERVES 2

1 tablespoon strawberry flavouring

170 ml (5½ fl oz/⅔ cup) cold milk

4 tablespoons cream

2 scoops strawberry ice cream

1 Blend the strawberry flavouring, cold milk, cream and ice cream in a blender until smooth. Serve in chilled glasses.

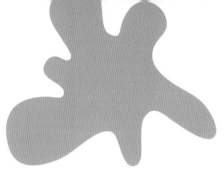

honey snaps

MAKES 24

125 g (4½ oz/½ cup) unsalted
  butter, softened

55 g (2 oz/¼ cup) caster (superfine) sugar

45 g (1¾ oz/¼ cup) soft brown sugar

115 g (4 oz/⅓ cup) honey

1 egg yolk

1 teaspoon natural vanilla extract

250 g (9 oz/2 cups) plain (all-purpose) flour

½ teaspoon bicarbonate of soda
  (baking soda)

125 g (4½ oz/1 cup) icing
  (confectioners') sugar

1–2 tablespoons lemon juice

1 Preheat the oven to 180°C (350°F/
   Gas 4). Line two baking trays with
   baking paper.

2 Cream the butter and caster and
   brown sugars in a bowl using electric
   beaters until fluffy. Add the honey,
   egg yolk and vanilla. Sift in the flour
   and bicarbonate of soda and stir to
   form a soft dough.

3 Shape tablespoons of the dough into
   circles. Place on the prepared trays
   and flatten slightly.

4 Bake for 10 minutes, or until golden.
   Cool on the trays for a few minutes,
   then transfer to a wire rack to cool.

5 To make the icing (frosting), place the
   icing sugar in a bowl. Add enough
   lemon juice until smooth. Spread the
   tops of the snaps with the icing.

custard dream stars

MAKES 30

185 g (6½ oz/¾ cup) unsalted
    butter, softened

40 g (1½ oz/⅓ cup) icing
    (confectioners') sugar

1 teaspoon natural vanilla extract

125 g (4½ oz/1 cup) plain
    (all-purpose) flour

40 g (1½ oz/⅓ cup) custard powder
    (instant vanilla pudding mix)

small coloured balls (cachous), to decorate

1. Preheat the oven to 180°C (350°F/ Gas 4). Line two baking trays with baking paper.

2. Cream the butter, sugar and vanilla in a bowl using electric beaters until pale and fluffy. Sift in the flour and custard powder and stir with a wooden spoon to form a soft dough, being careful not to overmix.

3. Transfer the mixture to a piping (icing) bag fitted with a 1.5 cm (5/8 inch) star nozzle. Pipe the mixture well apart onto the prepared baking trays to form star shapes, about 4 cm (1½ inches) in diameter.

4. Decorate each star with coloured balls. Refrigerate for 20 minutes.

5. Bake for 12–15 minutes, or until lightly golden. Allow to cool on the trays for a few minutes, then transfer to a wire rack to cool completely.

cream buns

MAKES 12

2 teaspoons dried yeast

2 tablespoons sugar

350 ml (12 fl oz) milk, warmed

435 g (15½ oz/3½ cups) plain (all-purpose) flour

60 g (2¼ oz) unsalted butter, melted

160 g (5¾ oz/½ cup) strawberry jam

310 ml (10¾ fl oz/1¼ cups) pouring (whipping) cream

1 tablespoon icing (confectioners') sugar

2 tablespoons icing (confectioners') sugar, extra, to dust

1 Put the yeast, 1 teaspoon of the sugar and the milk in a small bowl. Leave in a warm, draught-free place for 10 minutes, or until bubbles appear on the surface. The mixture should be frothy.

2 Sift the flour into a large bowl. Stir in ½ teaspoon salt and the remaining sugar. Make a well in the centre and add the milk mixture and butter and mix to a dough, first with a wooden spoon, then with your hands. Turn onto a lightly floured surface and knead for 10 minutes, or until smooth and elastic. Place in a lightly oiled bowl, cover with plastic wrap, and leave in a warm place for 1 hour, or until well risen.

3 Punch down the dough and turn onto a lightly floured surface. Knead for 2 minutes or until smooth. Divide into 12 pieces. Knead one portion at a time for 30 seconds on a lightly floured surface and then shape into a ball.

4 Preheat the oven to 210°C (415°F/Gas 6–7). Lightly grease two baking trays, dust lightly with flour and shake off any excess. Place the balls of dough, evenly spaced, on the trays. Set aside, covered with plastic wrap, in a warm place for 15 minutes, or until well risen.

5 Bake for 20 minutes or until well browned and cooked. Set aside for 5 minutes before transferring to a wire rack to cool completely. Using a serrated knife, make a slanted cut into the centre of each bun, to a depth of 5 cm (2 inches), from the top towards the base.

6 Spread jam over the cut base of each bun. Using electric beaters, beat the cream and icing sugar in a small bowl until firm peaks form. Spoon into a piping (icing) bag and pipe the whipped cream into the buns. Dust the tops with the extra icing sugar.

strawberry pillows

MAKES 18

155 g (5½ oz/1¼ cups) plain (all-purpose) flour

90 g (3¼ oz/⅓ cup) unsalted butter, chilled and cubed

90 g (3¼ oz/⅓ cup) sour cream

2 teaspoons finely grated lemon zest

80 g (2¾ oz/¼ cup) strawberry jam

1 egg, lightly beaten

1 tablespoon icing (confectioners') sugar, to dust

1 Line two baking trays with baking paper. Place the flour and butter in a food processor and process until it resembles coarse breadcrumbs. Add the sour cream and lemon zest and process until a dough forms.

2 Turn out onto a lightly floured work surface and press into a flat, round disc. Cover with plastic wrap and refrigerate for 30 minutes.

3 Preheat the oven to 200°C (400°F/Gas 6). Roll out the dough on a lightly floured work surface to 3 mm (⅛ inch) thick and, using a ruler, cut the dough into 6 cm (2½ inch) squares. Reshape any leftover dough, roll out and cut it into more squares.

4 Place ¾ teaspoon of the jam into the middle of each pastry square. Using the tip of your finger, wet the edges with a little water and fold the pastry in half, pressing to seal with a fork. Brush each pillow with a little of the beaten egg.

5 Place on the prepared trays and bake for 13 minutes, or until lightly golden. Allow to cool on the trays for a few minutes, then transfer to a wire rack to cool completely. Once cool, lightly dust with icing sugar.

Note: The strawberry pillows will keep, stored in an airtight container, for up to 5 days.

raspberry shortcake

SERVES 6

pastry

125 g (4½ oz/1 cup) plain (all-purpose) flour

40 g (1½ oz/⅓ cup) icing (confectioners') sugar

90 g (3¼ oz) unsalted butter, chilled and chopped

1 egg yolk

½ teaspoon natural vanilla extract

½–1 tablespoon iced water

topping

750 g (1 lb 10 oz/6 cups) fresh raspberries

30 g (1 oz/¼ cup) icing (confectioners') sugar

110 g (3¾ oz/⅓ cup) redcurrant jelly

whipped cream, to serve

1 To make the pastry, sift the flour and icing sugar into a large bowl. Using your fingertips, rub in the butter until the mixture resembles fine breadcrumbs. Add the egg yolk, vanilla extract and enough of the iced water to make the ingredients come together, then mix to a dough with a flat-bladed knife, using a cutting action. Turn out onto a lightly floured work surface and gather together into a ball. Flatten slightly, wrap in plastic wrap and refrigerate for 30 minutes.

2 Preheat the oven to 180°C (350°F/Gas 4). Roll out the pastry to fit six small 5 x 10 cm (2 x 4 inch) fluted loose-based flan (tart) tins and trim the edge. Prick all over with a fork and refrigerate for 20 minutes.

3 Line the pastry with baking paper and spread a layer of baking beads or uncooked rice evenly over the paper. Bake for 15–20 minutes, or until golden. Remove the paper and beads and bake for another 15 minutes. Cool on a wire rack.

4 To make the topping, set aside 500 g (1 lb 2 oz/4 cups) raspberries and mash the rest with the icing sugar. Spread the mashed raspberries over the shortcake just before serving.

5 Cover with the whole raspberries. Heat the redcurrant jelly in a small saucepan until melted and smooth. Use a soft pastry brush to coat the raspberries heavily with the warm redcurrant glaze. Cut into slices and serve with cream.

neenish tarts

MAKES 12

buttercream

60 g (2¼ oz) unsalted butter

60 g (2¼ oz/½ cup) icing (confectioners') sugar, sifted

1 tablespoon milk

1–2 drops natural vanilla extract

12 pre-cooked tartlet cases

2 tablespoons raspberry jam

125 g (4½ oz/1 cup) icing (confectioners') sugar, extra

1 teaspoon natural vanilla extract

3 teaspoons hot water

few drops pink food colouring

1 To make the buttercream, place the butter into a small bowl. Using electric beaters, beat on high speed for 1 minute. Add the sugar, milk and vanilla. Beat until light and creamy.

2 Place ½ teaspoon jam into each tartlet case and spread over the base. Top the jam with 2 teaspoons buttercream. Smooth the surface with the back of a teaspoon.

3 Sift the icing sugar into a small bowl. Make a well in the centre. Add the vanilla and water. Stir until the mixture is smooth. Divide the icing (frosting) into two portions. Leave one portion plain and tint the remaining portion pink.

4 Spread 1 teaspoon of plain icing over half of each tartlet and allow to set.

5 Spread 1 teaspoon of pink icing over the remaining half of each tartlet and allow to set.

in another galaxy

galactic discs

MAKES 12

12 small round honeysnap
    biscuits (cookies)

12 large white marshmallows

20 g (¾ oz) butter

sweets (candy), to decorate

1   Place a biscuit in each paper
patty case.

2   Place the marshmallows and butter in
a small heatproof bowl and set over
a saucepan of simmering water. Stir
until the mixture is smooth.

3   Spoon the mixture over the biscuits.
Decorate with clusters of sweets.
Refrigerate until set.

space slushy

SERVES 4–6

1 large large watermelon

250 g (9 oz) hulled strawberries

2 teaspoons caster (superfine) sugar

1 Peel and seed a large watermelon to give 2 kg (4 lb 8 oz) flesh and place in a bowl.

2 Add the hulled strawberries and caster sugar. Blend in batches in a blender or food processor until smooth, then pour into a shallow metal tray. Cover with plastic wrap and freeze for 2–3 hours, or until the mixture begins to freeze.

3 Remove from the freezer and return to the blender. Whiz quickly to break up the ice, pour into a pitcher and serve immediately.

space nuggets

MAKES 34

375 g (13 oz) boneless, skinless chicken thighs, roughly chopped

1 egg

1 tablespoon snipped chives

¼ teaspoon sesame oil

2 teaspoons plum sauce

1 teaspoon soy sauce

30 g (1 oz/1 cup) cornflakes

1 Preheat the oven to 180°C (350°F/Gas 4). Line a large baking tray with foil. Brush with melted butter or oil.

2 Place the chicken, egg, chives, sesame oil and sauces in a food processor. Process for 30 seconds or until the mixture is smooth.

3 Shape heaped teaspoons of the mixture into balls. Roll the balls in the cornflakes. Place the nuggets on the tray. Bake for 15 minutes, or until golden and crisp.

space spuds

MAKES 12

8 small cocktail potatoes

3 tablespoons sour cream

20 g (¾ oz) butter

1 egg

1 tablespoon mayonnaise

2 tablespoons snipped chives

3 bacon slices, chopped

60 g (2¼ oz/½ cup) grated cheddar cheese

chives, extra, to garnish

1 Preheat the oven to 180°C (350°F/Gas 4). Wrap the potatoes in foil. Bake for 30–40 minutes, or until tender.

2 Cut the potatoes in half and spoon out the flesh, leaving a thick shell. Keep the flesh. Combine the sour cream, butter, egg, mayonnaise, chives, bacon and reserved potato flesh in a small bowl. Mix well. Spoon the mixture into the potato shells. Place the potatoes on a baking tray.

3 Sprinkle with cheese and bake for 10 minutes, or until the cheese has melted. Garnish with extra chives.

mini galactic pizzas

MAKES 40

250 g (9 oz/2 cups) self-raising flour

100 g (3½ oz) butter, chopped

125 ml (4 fl oz/½ cup) buttermilk

2 tablespoons tomato paste (concentrated purée)

1 cabanossi stick, thinly sliced

1 small onion, thinly sliced

10 cherry tomatoes, thinly sliced

6 cheddar cheese slices, cut into 3 cm (1¼ inch) rounds

1 Preheat the oven to 180°C (350°F/Gas 4). Line two large baking trays with foil and grease.

2 Combine the flour and butter in a food processor. Process for 30 seconds or until the mixture is crumbly. Add the buttermilk. Process for 30 seconds.

3 Knead the dough on a floured surface until smooth. Roll the dough out to 3 mm (⅛ inch) thick. Cut into rounds using a 5 cm (2 inch) round cutter.

4 Place the rounds on the tray and spread with the tomato paste. Arrange the cabanossi, onion and tomato on top, then top with the cheese. Bake for 10 minutes, or until crisp.

chicken and corn bites

MAKES 50

185 g (6½ oz/1½ cups) self-raising flour

2 teaspoons chicken stock (bouillon) powder

½ teaspoon chicken seasoning salt

60 g (2¼ oz) butter, chopped

50 g (1¾ oz) corn chips, finely crushed

2 eggs, lightly beaten

chicken seasoning salt, extra, to sprinkle

1 Preheat the oven to 180°C (350°F/Gas 4). Line two baking trays with baking paper.

2 Sift the flour, stock powder and seasoning salt into a large bowl and add the butter. Rub into the flour with your fingertips until the mixture resembles fine breadcrumbs. Stir in the corn chips. Make a well in the centre, add the eggs and mix until the mixture comes together in beads.

3 Gently gather the dough together, lift out onto a lightly floured surface and press together into a ball. Roll out to 5 mm (¼ inch) thick.

4 Cut the dough into shapes with a plain or fluted cookie cutter. Place on the tray and sprinkle with the chicken salt. Bake for 15 minutes, or until lightly browned.

meteor ice cream cones

MAKES 8

500 ml (17 fl oz/2 cups) vanilla ice cream

8 round or square flat-based
ice cream cones

200 g (7 oz) small jubes (or other soft candy),
to decorate

150 g (5½ oz) dark chocolate melts, melted

1 Place 2 scoops of ice cream into each cone, packing it down firmly. Press the jubes into the ice cream. Place the cones in the freezer for 10 minutes to re-harden the ice cream.

2 Working with one cone at a time, spoon the melted chocolate over the ice cream. Drain off the excess chocolate and leave to set. Serve immediately or refreeze until ready to serve.

moon rock cakes

MAKES 18

250 g (9 oz/2 cups) self-raising flour

1 teaspoon mixed (pumpkin pie) spice

110 g (3¾ oz/½ cup) sugar

90 g (3¼ oz) unsalted butter, chopped

30 g (1 oz/¼ cup) sultanas (golden raisins)

2 tablespoons mixed peel
(mixed candied citrus peel)

1 egg

4 tablespoons milk

55 g (2 oz/¼ cup) sugar, extra

1 Preheat the oven to 180°C (350°F/Gas 4). Line two baking trays with baking paper.

2 Sift the flour and spice into a bowl. Add the sugar and butter. Rub in the butter until it resembles coarse breadcrumbs.

3 Mix in the sultanas and mixed peel. Make a well in the centre. Add the combined egg and milk and mix to form a soft dough.

4 Drop tablespoonfuls of dough onto the prepared trays, leaving room for spreading. Sprinkle lightly with extra sugar and bake for 10–15 minutes, or until golden.

camp out

coconut marshmallows

MAKES 16

220 g (7³/₄ oz/1 cup) sugar

1 tablespoon powdered gelatine

¹/₂ teaspoon coconut extract

90 g (3¹/₄ oz/1 cup) desiccated coconut

1 Line a deep 19 cm (7¹/₂ inch) square cake tin with foil.

2 Put the sugar, gelatine and 185 ml (6 fl oz/³/₄ cup) water in a small saucepan. Stir for 5 minutes. Simmer for another 5 minutes. Turn up the heat. Boil without stirring for another 5 minutes. Take the pan off the heat. Leave for 5 minutes, then beat for 5 minutes. Stir in the coconut extract.

3 Spread the mixture evenly in the tin. Leave for 1 hour to firm.

4 Put the coconut in a saucepan. Heat gently until golden. Take off the heat and cool. Cut the marshmallows in squares and toss in the coconut.

caramel popcorn balls

MAKES 50

2 tablespoons oil

¹/₂ cup popping corn

165 g (5³/₄ oz/³/₄ cup) sugar

85 g (2³/₄ oz) unsalted butter

2 tablespoons honey

2 tablespoons pouring (whipping) cream

1 Heat the oil in a large frying pan over medium heat. Add the popping corn and cover lightly. Hold the lid of the pan tightly and shake occasionally. Cook until the popping sounds stop. Put the popcorn into a large bowl. Set aside.

2 Combine the sugar, butter, honey and cream in a small heavy-based saucepan. Stir over medium heat without boiling until the sugar has completely dissolved. Brush sugar crystals from the sides of the pan with a wet pastry brush. Bring to the boil and boil for 5 minutes.

3 Pour the syrup over the popcorn. Using two metal spoons, combine with the popcorn. When the mixture has cooled enough to handle but has not set, form popcorn into balls about the size of a golf ball, using oiled hands. Place on a wire rack to set.

two-tone choc-chip cookies

MAKES ABOUT 40

125 g (4½ oz) butter

280 g (9 oz/1½ cups) soft brown sugar

2 teaspoons vanilla extract

2 eggs, lightly beaten

310 g (9¾ oz/2½ cups) plain (all-purpose)flour

1 teaspoon bicarbonate of soda (baking soda)

150 g (5½ oz) dark chocolate chips

150 g (5½ oz) white chocolate chips

1 Preheat the oven to 180°C (350°F/ Gas 4). Lightly grease two baking trays. Line with baking paper.

2 Using electric beaters, beat the butter, sugar and vanilla in a small bowl until light and creamy. Add the eggs gradually, beating well after each addition. Transfer to a large bowl.

3 Using a metal spoon, fold the sifted flour, soda and choc chips into the creamed mixture. Mix until smooth.

4 Drop level tablespoons of mixture onto the trays, allowing for spreading. Flatten the mixture slightly. Bake for 12–15 minutes or until lightly browned and cooked through. Transfer to a wire rack to cool.

Storage time: Choc-chip cookies can be stored in an airtight container for up to two weeks.

warm chocolate marshmallow drink

SERVES 2

500 ml (17 fl oz/2 cups) milk

2 tablespoons drinking chocolate, plus extra, to sprinkle

6 marshmallows

1 Put the milk in a saucepan and add the drinking chocolate. Stir over low heat until dissolved. When dissolved, turn up the heat until the chocolate is hot, then pour into mugs.

2 Top with marshmallows and sprinkle with chocolate.

roast vegetable bubble and squeak

MAKES 15

600 g (1 lb 6 oz) mixed roast vegetables (like potatoes, orange sweet potato, pumpkin/squash)

185 g (6½ oz) chopped cooked green vegetables (like brussels sprouts, peas, beans)

125 g (4½ oz) grated cheddar cheese

1 egg, lightly beaten

40 g (1½ oz) butter

1 Place the roast vegetables in a bowl and mash slightly with a fork or potato masher. Add the green vegetables, cheese and egg and stir until well combined. Season to taste.

2 Melt some of the butter in a frying pan and place six lightly greased egg rings in the pan. Spoon some vegetable mixture into each ring and press firmly.

3 Cook over medium heat for about 5 minutes on each side or until golden brown. Wipe the pan clean and repeat with the remaining vegetable mixture and butter.

corn and red capsicum tartlets

MAKES ABOUT 36

3 frozen puff pastry sheets, thawed

310 g (11 oz) tinned corn kernels, drained

150 g (5½ oz) red leicester cheese, grated

1 small red capsicum (pepper), finely chopped

2 eggs, lightly beaten

3 tablespoons buttermilk

170 ml (5½ fl oz/⅔ cup) thick (double/heavy) cream

1 teaspoon dijon mustard

dash Tabasco sauce

1 Preheat the oven to 200°C (400°F/Gas 6). Lightly grease three 12-hole round-based patty pans or mini muffin tins. Using a 6 cm (2½ inch) round pastry cutter, cut circles from the pastry sheets. Press the circles into the tins and prick the bases with a fork.

2 Combine the corn, cheese and capsicum in a bowl and season. Whisk the eggs, buttermilk, cream, mustard and Tabasco sauce.

3 Spoon some of the vegetable mixture into the pastry cases, then pour the egg mixture over the top until the cases are almost full. Bake for 20–25 minutes, or until set. Serve cold.

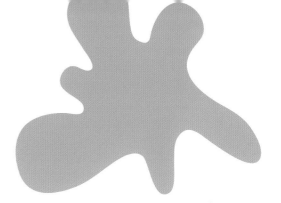

oven-baked potato wedges

MAKES 48

8 all-purpose potatoes

1 tablespoon oil

2 teaspoons seasoned salt

ready-made guacamole dip, to serve

1 Scrub the potatoes well and prick with a fork. Arrange them evenly around the turntable of the microwave and cook on HIGH [100%] for 20 minutes, turning over halfway through the cooking time. Leave to cool.

2 Preheat the oven to 240°C (475°F/Gas 8). Cut each potato into six wedges, carefully scooping out the flesh. (The flesh can be saved and reheated for mashed potato or bubble and squeak.)

3 Place the wedges in a single layer on a wire rack over a baking tray. Brush with oil on all sides and sprinkle with the seasoned salt.

4 Bake for 30 minutes, or until crisp.

chipolata sausages

MAKES 12

2 tablespoons virgin olive oil

2 red onions, cut into thin wedges

2 tablespoons dark brown sugar

3 teaspoons balsamic vinegar

12 chipolata sausages

12 par-baked mini bread rolls

100 g (3½ oz) cream cheese

100 g (3½ oz) rocket (arugula) leaves, stalks removed

1 Preheat the oven to 220°C (425°F/Gas 7). Heat 1½ tablespoons olive oil in a small saucepan. Add the onion and 1½ tablespoons water. Cover and cook over medium heat for about 10 minutes, stirring occasionally, until the onion is starting to brown. Stir in the sugar and vinegar and cook, uncovered, for 3 minutes, or until thick. Season and keep warm.

2 Heat the remaining oil in a large frying pan and cook the sausages in batches over medium–low heat for 6–8 minutes, or until brown and cooked. Remove and drain on crumpled paper towel.

3 Meanwhile, heat the bread rolls according to the manufacturer's instructions. When hot, slice lengthways, three-quarters of the way through, and spread with the cream cheese. Fill the rolls with rocket and a sausage, then onion.

Note: If you can't get chipolatas, you can use thin sausages and twist them through the centre.

mini pork quesadillas

MAKES 24

2¾ tablespoons olive oil

½ teaspoon ground oregano

1 teaspoon ground cumin

½ teaspoon garlic salt

350 g (12 oz) minced (ground) pork

30 g (1 oz/¼ cup) pitted black olives, sliced

55 g (2 oz/⅓ cup) green olives stuffed with red pimentos, sliced

2 tablespoons chopped coriander (cilantro) leaves

12 flour tortillas

60 g (2¼ oz/½ cup) grated mild cheddar cheese

75 g (2½ oz/½ cup) grated mozzarella cheese

coriander (cilantro) sprigs, to garnish

1 To make the pork mixture, heat 1½ tablespoons of the olive oil in a large frying pan. Add the oregano, cumin, and garlic salt and cook for 30 seconds. Add the pork and cook over high heat for 10 minutes, then add the olives. Cook for another 5 minutes, then stir in the chopped coriander. Remove from the heat and allow to cool.

2 Cut each tortilla in half. Place 1 tablespoon of the filling on one half of each half. Mix the cheeses together, then put 1 tablespoon of the grated cheese on top of the spicy pork mixture. Turn the flap of tortilla over the filling and press down firmly.

3 Heat 2 teaspoons of the remaining oil in a non-stick frying pan over high heat. Cook the quesadillas in batches of six for 3–4 minutes each side, or until golden. Add a teaspoon of oil to the pan after each batch. Garnish with coriander sprigs.

halloween

scary face pikelets

MAKES 24

220 g (7¾ oz) packet pikelet (griddle cake) mix

60 g (2¼ oz) dark chocolate, chopped

50 g (1¾ oz) butter

1 Prepare the pikelet batter according to the instructions on the packet. Leave to stand for 10 minutes.

2 Place the chocolate in a small heatproof bowl and set over a saucepan of simmering water, making sure the bowl doesn't touch the water. Stir until the chocolate has melted and the mixture is smooth. Spoon the chocolate into a small icing (piping) bag.

3 Heat a small amount of butter over medium heat in a large non-stick frying pan. Pipe a small scary face with chocolate mixture on the base of the pan. Carefully spoon a tablespoon of pikelet batter over the face. Cook until bubbles appear on the surface. (This will be about 30 seconds.) Turn and cook other side.

4 Remove from the pan. Repeat with the remaining chocolate and pikelet mixture. Serve warm or cold.

mouse traps

MAKES 10

10 bread slices

60 g (2¼ oz) butter, softened

10 ham slices

250 g (9 oz) cheddar cheese, finely grated

3 tablespoons tomato sauce (ketchup)

1 Preheat the grill (broiler) to high. Toast the bread lightly on both sides.

2 Spread one side of each piece of bread thinly with butter. Place a slice of ham on each piece of bread and sprinkle with grated cheese. Spoon 2 teaspoons of tomato sauce in the centre of the bread.

3 Place the bread under the preheated grill and cook for 1–2 minutes, or until the cheese melts and the tomato sauce spreads slightly. Serve hot.

monster crush

SERVES 4–6

750 ml (26 fl oz/ 3 cups) apple and
blackcurrant juice

500 ml (17 fl oz/2 cups) soda water
(club soda)

1 tablespoon caster (superfine) sugar

150 g (5½ oz) blueberries

ice cubes, to serve

1 Place the apple and blackcurrant juice, soda water, sugar and blueberries into a blender and blend until smooth.

2 Serve in chilled glasses over ice.

Note: If you have a really good blender, you may wish to add the ice cubes when blending the other ingredients to make a slushy.

chocolate spiders

MAKES 24

340 g (11¾ oz) packet chocolate cake mix

100 g (3½ oz) dark chocolate

30 g (1 oz) butter

4 licorice straps

24 red smarties

grated chocolate, to sprinkle

1 Preheat the oven to the temperature recommended on the cake-mix packet. Grease 24 shallow patty pans. Make the cake mix according to the directions on the packet. Fill each patty cup two-thirds full with cake mixture. Bake for 10–15 minutes, or until cooked. Cool on a wire rack. Place a baking tray under the rack.

2 Combine the chocolate and butter in a small heatproof bowl set over a saucepan of simmering water until the chocolate and butter have melted and the mixture is smooth. Remove from the heat and mix well.

3 Spoon the chocolate over the cakes, ensuring that each cake is completely covered. Allow the chocolate to set.

4 Cut the licorice straps into thin lengths 3 cm (1¼ inches) long. Attach eight of these lengths to each cake as spiders' legs. Cut the smarties in half and place on the spiders for the eyes. Sprinkle the cakes with grated chocolate to make furry bodies.

witches' concoction

1 packet green or blackcurrant jelly (gelatin dessert) crystals (you can use any colour you like)

assorted sweets (candy), like snakes and frogs

1 Make the jelly according to the packet instructions. Pour into a large glass bowl or small individual glasses.

2 Add the sweets and refrigerate until set.

zombie brain meatballs

MAKES ABOUT 10

850 g (1 lb 14 oz) minced (ground) lamb

1 small onion, finely chopped

3 tablespoons finely chopped parsley

1 tablespoon dijon mustard

1 Place the lamb, onion, parsley and mustard in a large bowl and mix to combine.

2 Roll level tablespoonfuls of mixture into 40 balls. Refrigerate until needed. Thread four meatballs onto each of the skewers.

3 Heat a frying pan over medium–high heat and brush lightly with oil. Cook the meatball skewers for about 12 minutes until well browned all over. Drain on paper towel.

bugs in rugs

MAKES 12

12 cocktail frankfurts

3 white bread slices, crusts removed

3 tablespoons melted butter

2 tablespoons poppy seeds

1 Preheat the oven to 180°C (350°F/Gas 4). Pierce the frankfurts all over with a fork. Cut each slice of bread into quarters. Place a frankfurt across each piece. Bring up the edges and secure with a toothpick. Brush with the butter and sprinkle with poppy seeds.

2 Place on a baking tray. Bake for 10–15 minutes, or until the bread is crisp and brown. Remove from the oven. Remove toothpicks before serving.

bleeding ghoul gut pies

MAKES 24

6 ready-rolled shortcrust (pie) pastry sheets

1 tablespoon oil

1 onion, chopped

2 garlic cloves, crushed

500 g (1 lb 2 oz) minced (ground) beef

2 tablespoons plain (all-purpose) flour

375 ml (13 fl oz/1½ cups) beef stock

4 tablespoons tomato sauce (ketchup)

2 teaspoons worcestershire sauce

½ teaspoon dried mixed herbs

2 small tomatoes, cut in half and sliced

½ teaspoon dried oregano leaves

extra tomato sauce (ketchup), to serve

1 Preheat the oven to 200°C (400°F/Gas 6).

2 Cut the pastry into 24 circles using a 7 cm (2¾ inch) round cutter. Press the circles into two lightly greased 12-hole patty pans or mini muffin tins.

3 Heat the oil in a heavy-based saucepan, add the onion and garlic and cook over medium heat for 2 minutes, or until the onion is soft. Add the beef and stir over high heat for 3 minutes, or until well browned and all the liquid has evaporated.

4 Add the flour, stir until combined, then cook over medium heat for 1 minute. Add the stock, sauces and herbs and stir over low heat until boiling. Reduce the heat to low and simmer for 5 minutes until reduced and thickened, stirring occasionally. Allow to cool.

5 Divide the filling among the pastry circles. Top each with two half slices of tomato and sprinkle with oregano. Bake for 25 minutes, or until the pastry is golden brown and crisp. Cover with tomato sauce and serve hot.

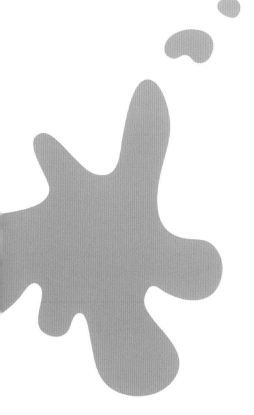

easter egg hunt

bunny and duck cookies

MAKES ABOUT 12

125 g (4½ oz/½ cup) unsalted butter,
cubed and softened

115 g (4 oz/½ cup) caster (superfine) sugar

2 egg yolks

2 teaspoons finely grated lemon zest

155 g (5½ oz/1¼ cups) plain
(all-purpose) flour

110 g (3¾ oz/¾ cup) coarse cornmeal

coloured sugar or sprinkles, to dust

1 Preheat the oven to 160°C (315°F/
Gas 2–3). Line a baking tray with
baking paper.

2 Cream the butter andcaster sugar in
a bowl using electric beaters until
pale and fluffy. Add the egg yolks
and lemon zest, beating until just
combined. Sift in the flour, add the
cornmeal and stir to form a soft dough.

3 Turn the dough out onto a floured
surface and knead until the mixture
comes together. Roll out the dough
between two pieces of baking paper
to 1 cm (½ inch) thick.

4 Cut the dough into shapes using
rabbit and duck cookie cutters.

5 Place on the trays well apart and bake
for 15–20 minutes, or until lightly
golden around the edges. Allow to
cool on the trays for a few minutes,
then transfer to a wire rack, dust
with icing sugar and leave to cool.

banana shake

SERVES 2

3 passionfruit, halved

1 large banana, chopped

250 ml (9 fl oz/1 cup) skim milk

60 g (2¼ oz/¼ cup) low-fat plain yoghurt

1 Scoop out the passionfruit pulp and place in a blender. Add the banana, milk and yoghurt and pulse until smooth. (Add more milk if it is too thick.)

2 Pour into two glasses and serve immediately.

vegie puffs

MAKES 12

1 potato, peeled and finely chopped

1 carrot, finely chopped

1 zucchini (courgette), peeled and chopped

1 celery stalk, chopped

40 g (1½ oz/¼ cup) chopped pumpkin (squash)

30 g (1 oz/¼ cup) chopped broccoli

30 g (1 oz/¼ cup) chopped cauliflower

250 g (9 oz/2 cups) grated tasty cheese

1 sheet puff pastry, thawed, cut in half

milk, for coating

1 Put the potato, carrot, zucchini, celery, pumpkin, broccoli and cauliflower in a small saucepan and add enough water to cover. Bring to the boil, then reduce the heat and simmer for 3 minutes. Drain well and transfer to a bowl to cool. Add the cheese to the vegetables and mix well.

2 Preheat the oven to 220°C (425°F/Gas 7). Put the two pieces of pastry out on a board, divide the mixture in half and spread it along the long side of each piece.

3 Roll up the pastry to form a sausage shape, brush the edge with a little milk and press to seal. Place, seam side down, on a cutting board.

4 Cut each roll into six even-sized pieces using a sharp knife. Make a small slit in the centre of each and place on a lightly greased baking tray. Brush with milk and bake for 10 minutes or until crisp and golden.

mini scones with ham and cheese

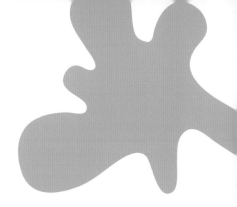

MAKES ABOUT 40

250 g (9 oz/2 cups) plain (all-purpose) flour

3 teaspoons baking powder

110 g (3¾ oz) butter

100 g (3½ oz) stilton cheese

2 tablespoons snipped chives

185 ml (6 fl oz/¾ cup) milk

filling

4 tablespoons dijon mustard

150 g (5½ oz) shaved ham

100 g (3½ oz) cheddar cheese

1 Sift the flour, baking powder and ¾ teaspoon salt into a bowl. Grate the butter and cheese into the flour and rub in using your fingertips. Stir in the chives. Pour in the milk and combine with a fork until large clumps form. Turn onto a floured surface and press into a ball.

2 Preheat the oven to 220°C (425°F/Gas 7). Roll the dough out on a floured surface into a 15 x 25 cm (6 x 10 inch) rectangle. With the long edge of the dough facing you, fold in both ends so they meet in the centre, then fold the dough in half widthways. Roll again into a 15 x 25 cm (6 x 10 inch) rectangle, about 1 cm (½ inch) thick.

3 Cut rounds close together with a 3 cm (1¼ inch) cutter. Push the scraps together and roll and cut as before. Place 2.5 cm (1 inch) apart on a baking tray and refrigerate for 20 minutes. Bake for 10–12 minutes.

4 Cut the scones in half. Spread the bases with the mustard. Put a folded piece of ham on each bottom half, top with cheese, then replace the tops.

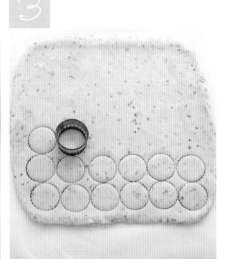

chocolate fudge sandwiches

MAKES ABOUT 20

250 g (9 oz/2 cups) plain (all-purpose) flour

30 g (1 oz/¼ cup) unsweetened cocoa powder

200 g (7 oz) unsalted butter, chilled and diced

100 g (3½ oz) icing (confectioners') sugar

2 egg yolks, lightly beaten

1 teaspoon natural vanilla extract

filling

100 g (3½ oz/⅔ cup) dark chocolate, chopped

1 tablespoon golden syrup or dark corn syrup

25 g (1 oz) unsalted butter, softened

1 Preheat the oven to 200°C (400°F/Gas 6). Lightly grease two baking trays.

2 Sift the flour and cocoa powder into a bowl and rub in the butter. Sift in the icing sugar and stir to combine. Stir in the egg yolks and vanilla until a dough forms.

3 Transfer the dough to a floured work surface and shape into a 4 x 6 x 26 cm (1½ x 2½ x 10½ inch) block. Wrap in plastic wrap and chill for 30 minutes. Cut the dough into 40–48 slices, about 5 mm (¼ inch) wide. Place the slices on the baking trays. Bake for 10 minutes, or until firm. Cool on the trays for 5 minutes, then transfer to a wire rack to cool.

4 To make the filling, put the chocolate in a heatproof bowl and set over a saucepan of simmering water, stirring until melted. Remove from the heat, stir in the golden syrup and butter and continue stirring until smooth. Allow to cool a little, then chill for 10 minutes.

5 Use the chocolate to sandwich two biscuits together.

chocolate hot cross buns

MAKES 12 BUNS

1 tablespoon dried yeast or 30 g (1 oz) fresh yeast

500 g (1 lb 2 oz/4 cups) white strong flour

2 tablespoons caster (superfine) sugar

1 teaspoon mixed (pumpkin pie) spice

1 teaspoon ground cinnamon

40 g (1½ oz) butter

100 g (3½ oz) milk chocolate chips

paste for crosses

30 g (1 oz/¼ cup) plain (all-purpose) flour

¼ teaspoon caster (superfine) sugar

glaze

1½ tablespoons caster (superfine) sugar

1 teaspoon powdered gelatine

1 Lightly grease a baking tray. Put the yeast, 2 teaspoons of the flour, 1 teaspoon of the sugar and 125 ml (4 fl oz/½ cup) warm water in a small bowl and stir well. Leave in a warm, draught-free place for 10 minutes, or until bubbles appear on the surface.

2 Sift the remaining flour and spices into a large bowl and stir in the sugar. Using your fingertips, rub in the butter. Stir in the chocolate chips. Make a well in the centre, stir in the yeast mixture and up to 185 ml (6 fl oz/¾ cup) water to make a soft dough.

3 Turn the dough out onto a floured surface and knead for 5 minutes, or until smooth, adding more flour if needed, to prevent sticking. Place the dough in a floured bowl, cover with plastic wrap and leave in a warm place for 30–40 minutes, or until doubled in size.

4 Preheat the oven to 200°C (400°F/Gas 6). Turn the dough out onto a lightly floured surface and knead gently to deflate. Divide into 12 portions and roll each into a ball.

5 Place the balls on the tray, just touching each other, in a rectangle three rolls wide and four rolls long. Cover loosely with plastic wrap or a damp tea towel and leave in a warm place for 20 minutes, or until nearly doubled in size.

6 To make the crosses, mix the flour, sugar and 2½ tablespoons water into a paste. Spoon into a paper piping (icing) bag and pipe crosses on top of the buns. Bake for 20 minutes, or until golden brown.

7 To make the glaze, put the sugar, gelatine and 1 tablespoon water in a saucepan and stir over the heat until dissolved. Brush over the hot buns and leave to cool.

custard tarts

MAKES 12

150 g (5½ oz/1¼ cups) plain (all-purpose) flour

25 g (1 oz) white vegetable shortening (Copha), chopped and softened

30 g (1 oz) unsalted butter, chopped and softened

220 g (7¾ oz/1 cup) sugar

500 ml (17 fl oz/2 cups) milk

30 g (1 oz/¼ cup) cornflour (cornstarch)

1 tablespoon custard powder or instant vanilla pudding mix

4 egg yolks

1 teaspoon natural vanilla extract

1 Sift the flour into a bowl and add 185 ml (6 fl oz/¾ cup) water, or enough to form a soft dough.

2 Gather the dough into a ball, then roll out on baking paper to form a 24 x 30 cm (9½ x 12 inch) rectangle. Spread the Copha over the surface. Roll up from the short edge to form a log. Roll the dough out into a rectangle again and spread with the butter. Roll up again into a roll and slice into 12 even pieces.

3 Use your fingertips to press each round out to a circle large enough to cover the base and side of 12 muffin holes. Press into the holes and refrigerate.

4 Put the sugar and 4 tablespoons water in a saucepan and stir over low heat. Stir a little of the milk with the cornflour and custard powder in a bowl. Add to the pan with the remaining milk, egg yolks and vanilla. Stir over low heat until thick. Cover and cool. Preheat the oven to 220°C (425°F/Gas 7).

5 Pour the filling into the pastry cases. Bake for about 25–30 minutes.

north pole

white chocolate fondue with fruit

SERVES 6–8

125 ml (4 fl oz/½ cup) light corn syrup

170 ml (5½ fl oz/⅔ cup) thick (double/heavy) cream

250 g (9 oz) white chocolate, chopped

marshmallows and fresh fruit, such as sliced peaches, strawberries and cherries

1 Combine the corn syrup and cream in a small saucepan or fondue set. Bring to the boil, then remove from the heat.

2 Add 3 tablespoons water and the white chocolate and stir until melted. Serve with marshmallows and fresh fruit. Allow your guests to help themselves by dipping their choice of fruit in the white chocolate fondue. Use skewers or long forks as the fondue can be quite hot.

rudolph's punch

SERVES 10

660 g (1 lb 7 oz/3 cups) sugar

850 ml (28 fl oz) pineapple juice

250 ml (9 fl oz/1 cup) orange juice

juice of 2 large lemons

pulp of 2 passionfruit

1.25 litres (44 fl oz/5 cups) cold black tea

500 ml (17 fl oz/2 cups) dry ginger ale

ice cubes, to serve

apples, peaches and other fresh fruit in season, to garnish

mint sprigs, to garnish

1 Combine 750 ml (26 fl oz/3 cups) water and the sugar in a large saucepan. Stir over medium heat until the sugar dissolves. Bring to the boil, then reduce the heat. Simmer for 10 minutes. Remove from the heat to cool.

2 When cool, transfer to a large punch bowl and add the pineapple juice, orange juice, lemon juice, passionfruit pulp, tea and dry ginger ale. Add the ice. Garnish with fresh fruit and mint sprigs.

frankfurt bonbons

MAKES 12

12 small cocktail frankfurts

3 ready-rolled puff pastry sheets

1 egg, lightly beaten

cotton or jute string

1 Preheat the oven to 180°C (350°F/Gas 4). Line two baking trays with foil. Brush with melted butter or oil.

2 Prick the frankfurts with a fork. Cut each pastry sheet into four squares. Brush each square with beaten egg. Place a frankfurt on each pastry square and roll up. Gently press the edges together.

3 Carefully pinch in the ends of the pastry. Tie the ends loosely with pieces of string. Cut a fringe in the ends, using scissors.

4 Place the pastries on the trays. Brush lightly with the beaten egg. Bake for 15 minutes or until golden.

cheese ribbons

MAKES ABOUT 30

2 ready-rolled puff pastry sheets

tomato sauce or Vegemite

125 g (4½ oz/1 cup) grated cheddar cheese

1 Preheat the oven to 220°C (425°F/Gas 7). Spread one sheet of pastry with tomato sauce or Vegemite and sprinkle with cheese.

2 Put the second piece of pastry on top and press the edges to seal.

3 Cut into 1 cm (¾ inch) strips, then cut each strip into three pieces. Twist and put on a lightly greased baking tray.

4 Bake for 10 minutes, or until golden and puffed. Cool on a wire rack.

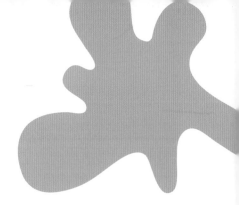

cathedral window cookies

MAKES 30

200 g (7 oz) unsalted butter

170 g (6 oz/³⁄₄ cup) caster (superfine) sugar

1 egg, lightly beaten

1 teaspoon natural vanilla extract

1 tablespoon milk

1 teaspoon baking powder

310 g (11 oz/2¹⁄₂ cups) plain (all-purpose) flour

4 tablespoons crushed green boiled sweets (candy)

4 tablespoons crushed red boiled sweets (candy)

4 tablespoons crushed yellow boiled sweets (candy)

1 Preheat the oven to 180°C (350°F/Gas 4). Line two baking trays with baking paper. Using electric beaters, beat the butter and sugar in a bowl until creamy. Add the egg and beat. Add the vanilla and milk and beat until combined. Transfer the mixture to a bowl. Fold in the sifted baking powder and flour. Stir until smooth.

2 Turn the dough onto a floured surface. Knead for about 1 minute. Divide the dough in two and shape into balls. Cover with plastic wrap and refrigerate for 1 hour. Roll one portion of the dough to a 3 mm (¹⁄₈ inch) thickness. Using a pastry wheel, cut the dough into 6 x 8 cm (2¹⁄₂ x 3¹⁄₄ inch) rectangles.

3 Place on the trays. Use small fluted cutters to cut out windows in the middle of the cookies. Fill the spaces with crushed boiled sweets, level with the surface of the cookie. Bake for 15 minutes. Remove from the oven and stand on the tray for 2 minutes before transferring with the baking paper to a wire rack to cool.

snowmen

MAKES 10

2 litres (70 fl oz/8 cups) vanilla ice cream

10 pink and white marshmallows

65 g (2¼ oz/¾ cup) desiccated coconut

10 thin strips of red sour straps

20 smarties

4 red glacé cherries, cut into quarters

1 Using a large ice-cream scoop, place 10 scoops of ice cream on a flat tray. Make 10 more scoops using a smaller scoop. Place these on top of the large scoops. Freeze for 30 minutes until very firm.

2 To make the marshmallows into hats, use a small round cutter to cut smaller circles. Press these onto the large marshmallows and flatten slightly.

3 Remove the ice cream from the freezer, roll in the coconut and top each with a marshmallow hat. Tie the sour strap around the neck to form a scarf. Use the smarties for eyes. Make a mouth with a glacé cherry piece. Return to the freezer until ready to serve.

spiced christmas muffins

MAKES 12

325 g (11½ oz/1¾ cups) mixed dried fruit

310 g (11 oz/2½ cups) self-raising flour

1 teaspoon mixed (pumpkin pie) spice

1 teaspoon ground cinnamon

½ teaspoon freshly grated nutmeg

155 g (5½ oz/⅔ cup) soft brown sugar

125 ml (4 fl oz/½ cup) milk

1 egg, lightly beaten

2 tablespoons apricot jam

½ teaspoon very finely grated lemon zest

½ teaspoon very finely grated orange zest

125 g (4½ oz) unsalted butter, melted and cooled

125 g (4½ oz) soft ready-made icing (frosting)

icing (confectioners') sugar, to dust

2 tablespoons apricot jam, extra, warmed and sieved

red and green glacé cherries, for decoration

1 Put the dried fruit and 4 tablespoons water in a bowl. Cover and marinate, stirring often, for 1–2 hours.

2 Preheat the oven to 200°C (400°F/Gas 6). Line 12 standard muffin holes with paper patty cases. Sift the flour, mixed spice, cinnamon and nutmeg into a large bowl and stir in the brown sugar. Make a well in the centre.

3 Combine the milk, egg, apricot jam, lemon and orange zest and melted butter in a bowl and pour into the well. Stir in the dried fruit mixture. Fold gently.

4 Divide the mixture evenly among the muffin holes. Bake for 20 minutes. Cool in the tins for 5 minutes, then transfer to a wire rack to cool.

5 Place the icing on a work surface dusted with a little icing sugar. Roll out to 2 mm (⅛ inch) thick. Using a 7 cm (2¾ inch) fluted round cutter, cut out 12 rounds.

6 Brush the muffins with the extra apricot jam and top each with a round of icing. Decorate with red glacé cherries and small 'leaves' of green glacé cherries.

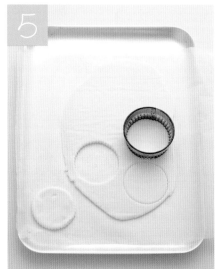

gingerbread christmas tree

MAKES 1 TREE ABOUT 25 CM (10 INCHES) HIGH

125 g (4½ oz) unsalted butter

115 g (4 oz/½ cup) caster (superfine) sugar

1 egg yolk

3 tablespoons honey

250 g (9 oz/2 cups) plain (all-purpose) flour

1 teaspoon bicarbonate of soda (baking soda)

2 teaspoons ground ginger

mixed coloured balls (cachous)

1 egg white

185 g (6½ oz/1½ cups) icing (confectioners') sugar

5 ice cream cones

icing (confectioners') sugar, extra, for dusting

1 Preheat the oven to 180°C (350°F/Gas 4). Brush two baking trays with melted butter or oil. Using electric beaters, beat the butter and caster sugar in a bowl until light and creamy. Add the egg yolk and honey and beat until combined.

2 Add the sifted flour, soda and ginger. Press together to form a soft dough. Turn onto a lightly floured surface. Knead for 1 minute until smooth. Cover with plastic wrap and refrigerate for 15 minutes.

3 Roll the dough out between two sheets of baking paper to about 3 mm (⅛ inch) thick. Cut 30 Christmas tree shapes from the dough using an 8 cm (3¼ inch) cutter. Cut six star shapes from the remaining dough, using a 4 cm (1½ inch) cutter. Place on the trays, allowing room to spread. Press the coloured balls onto the top of each tree and onto one point of each star. Bake for 15 minutes. Cool on a wire rack.

4 Using electric beaters, beat the egg white until slightly frothy. Add the sifted icing sugar, 1 tablespoon at a time, beating until smooth. Add enough icing sugar to give a stiff spreading consistency.

5 To assemble the tree, stack cones on top of each other, spreading a little icing between each to join them together. Starting with the bottom cone, spread icing thickly around it. Press the Christmas tree and star biscuits into the icing, stacking biscuits in overlapping layers around the cone. Work your way up the cones in this manner, spreading with icing as you go. Leave room at the top, and spread with icing. Press two stars, standing upright back to back, on the top. Sift the extra icing sugar over the tree.

party games

Balloon games

Balloon fight

Give every child a balloon labelled with their name. Children throw their balloon into the air and try to keep it there, while at the same time trying to knock other balloons to the ground. The winner is the last player with a balloon in the air.

Balloon volleyball

Tie a piece of string across the room or play area, at about head height. Divide the players into two teams and position them on either side of the string. One team serves by hitting the balloon over the string and the other team must return the balloon without letting it fall to the ground. If the balloon hits the ground, the other team scores a point. The first team to score 20 is the winner. This is a good indoor game if the weather is bad. Make sure you clear any breakables away.

Broomstick relay

Mark two parallel lines about 3 metres apart, and call one the starting line. Divide the children into pairs, then line them up facing each other behind the lines. Each child at the starting line has a broom and a balloon. The child must sweep the balloon towards their opposite number, who must then sweep it back again. Bursting balloons disqualify sweepers, and the first pair to successfully complete the relay wins.

Hunting & hiding games

Scavenger Hunt

Give each player a list of objects to find and collect within a certain length of time, such as 30 minutes. For children who read well, write the list on a paper bag, which can then be used for collecting the items. You can decide whether to include theme-related objects that you have 'planted' around the party area, or ordinary objects lying around your house and garden. The first to collect all the items on the list is the winner. A simple scavenger list might include items like a piece of string, a flower, a leaf, a stone, a feather and so on.

Storybook partners

Before the party, make a list of storybook partners like Little Red Riding Hood and the Wolf, Alice in Wonderland and the White Rabbit, Cinderella and Prince Charming, Hansel and Gretel, Jack and the Giant, and so on. Write each name on a piece of paper. At the start of the game, pin a name on the back of each child, not allowing them to see their storybook name. Each child must find out who he or she is, by asking the other players questions like 'Am I an animal?' What colour am I?'. Answers should be given in the form of clues without giving away the storybook name. Once all the children have guessed correctly, they search for their storybook partners.

Sardines

All the children except one count to 20 while the odd one out goes into hiding. When they reach 20, the children must hunt for the missing child. Whoever finds the child has to join him or her in hiding. Eventually all but one child will be squashed into the hiding place. When the last child discovers the hiding place, the game can be played again with the child who found the hiding place first taking a turn as the next hider.

Captives

Divide the children into two teams, the Sheriffs and the Bandits. Sheriffs cover their eyes and count to 100 while the Bandits scatter throughout the house and hide. The Sheriffs then seek out all those in hiding. When a Sheriff finds a Bandit, he or she is taken captive and put in a 'jailhouse' nominated at the beginning of the game. The first captured Bandit must hold onto the jailhouse bars (the leg of a table or the side of a chair) with one hand. The next captive must hold hands with the first. Each captive holds hands with the last, so that the captives form a chain. Meanwhile, those Bandits who are still in hiding have to sneak back to the jailhouse and free the captives as quietly as possible. A Bandit may free only one captive at a time, and must free the captive who is last in the chain. A captive is freed by a touch on the shoulder. Once free, Bandits go off to hide again. The object of the game is for the Sheriffs to capture all the Bandits.

Blindfold games

Blindfold drawing

Give each blindfolded player a piece of paper and a pencil, and a subject to draw that is related to the party's theme. When the players think they have completed their drawing, ask for some additions to be made, for example, 'Put a pom-pom on the clown's hat'. The winning picture is the one voted the funniest or the best by the other players.

Pin the tail on the donkey

Draw an outline of a tailless donkey on a large sheet of paper. Mark a large cross where the tail should be attached. Hang up the picture at the children's eye level and give the first child a paper or rope donkey's tail with a drawing pin in one end. Blindfold the child, spin them around three times and point him in the general direction of the donkey. Mark the spot the child has chosen to place the tail with the child's initials and go on to the next child. The one who puts the tail on, or nearest to, the correct spot wins. You can also adapt this game to your theme, for example, Pin the Tail on the Stegasaurus, Pin the Tail on the Zebra, or Pin the Tail on the Teddy Bear.

Blindman's Bluff

Blindfold one child and spin them around three times. The other players must move around making noise and so on while the blindfolded player tries to catch them. When they catch a child, they must guess who it is. If they guess correctly, the caught child takes over as the blind man.

Musical games

Hot potato

The children sit in a circle. They pass around a ball as the music plays. When the music stops, the child holding the ball is eliminated from the circle. The last child left in the circle is the winner.

Musical chairs

Make two lines of back-to-back chairs. There should be one less chair than the number of children. When the music starts, children march around the chairs. When the music stops, everyone sits down. The person without a chair drops out of the game. Remove another chair and start the music again. The last child left is the winner.

Musical bumps

The children dance as the music plays. When the music stops, all players must sit down. The last one to sit is out. The last child left is the winner.

Musical statues

The children dance as the music plays. When the music stops, all players must freeze and remain as still as statues. Anyone who moves is out. The last child left wins.

Pass the parcel

Wrap a prize in many layers of newspaper. The children sit in a circle and pass the parcel to each other as the music plays. When the music stops, the child holding the parcel can unwrap a layer. The music starts again. Eventually the music stops for the last layer of wrapping, leaving the winner holding the prize.

Memory games

I went to Mars

The children sit in a circle. The first child announces 'I went to Mars and I took a…' then names any object. For example, the child might say: 'I went to Mars and I took a bicycle.' The next child has to repeat this and add another object to the list. For example: 'I went to Mars and I took a bicycle and a parrot.' The third child will add a new object, always keeping the list in order. The game continues around the circle for as long as possible. This game can be adapted to most themes such as 'I asked the fairy for a…', or 'I went on a camping trip and I took a…' or 'I asked the pirate for a…', etc.

Paddy's black pig

This is great fun for a small group of children. The group is asked questions to which they can only give one answer: 'Paddy's black pig'. Any child who smiles or giggles is out. Ask questions that will trick them into laughing such as 'Who did you see when you looked in the mirror this morning?', or 'Who's your best friend?'.

Indoor games

Hat making

This is a quiet game for a small number of children and works very well when played in pairs. Give each pair one newspaper, three sheets of coloured paper, some pins, a wad of blu-tack, a roll of sticky tape, a pair of scissors and any other craft materials you like, such as pipe cleaners, stickers, glitter, and markers. The pairs are asked to make a fancy hat in 15 minutes, using only the given material. The winning hat is the one voted the best by all the players.

Trivia quiz

You can choose general subjects or limit them to the party theme. Set up a scoreboard with the names of the players on it. Children can also play in pairs. Read out the questions and get the answer from the first child whose hand shoots up. You can award first, second and third place prizes.

Outdoor games & races

Sack race

Give each child a hessian sack or large pillowcase. The children must line up at the starting line and jump to the finish line, holding the sack around themselves. The first child to reach the finish line wins.

Egg and spoon race

Give each child a hard-boiled egg and a spoon. They must hold their egg, balanced on the spoon, while running from the start line to the finish line. If they drop their egg they must put it back on the spoon, go back to the start line and begin again. The first child to the finish line is the winner.

Teddyback race

Children line up on all fours at the start line. Place a teddy bear on each child's back. The teddy bear must be carried to the finish line without it falling off. If a teddy bear falls, its owner must pick it up, return to the start line, and begin again. The first child to the finish line is the winner.

Three-legged race

Divide the children into pairs. Use a scarf or large handkerchief to tie the right leg of one child to the left leg of the other child. The pair must race as one three-legged person from the start to finish line.

Games of trickery & suprise

The Captain's coming

Nominate one side of the room to be port, and another to be starboard. Also nominate places to be a rowboat, the anchor, the cannon and so on. The children form a group. Call out a command, for example, 'The Captain's coming — scrub the decks!' The last child to obey the command is out. Other commands could be to lift the anchor or run to the rowboat.

Grandmother

One child is 'Grandmother'. All the other children stand in line some distance away. Grandmother stands with her back to the children. The children must creep forward towards her. Whenever Grandmother quickly turns around, they must freeze. If she sees any of them moving, they must return to the start. The first to reach Grandmother becomes the new Grandmother.

Simon says

The children face 'Simon', who gives an instruction that begins with 'Simon says'. The children must only follow instructions which begin with 'Simon says'. Players who make a mistake are out.

index

Published in 2009 by Murdoch Books Pty Limited

Murdoch Books Australia
Pier 8/9
23 Hickson Road
Millers Point NSW 2000
Phone: +61 (0) 2 8220 2000
Fax: +61 (0) 2 8220 2558
www.murdochbooks.com.au

Murdoch Books UK Limited
Erico House
6th Floor
93–99 Upper Richmond Road
Putney, London SW15 2TG
Phone: +44 (0) 20 8785 5995
Fax: +44 (0) 20 8785 5985
www.murdochbooks.co.uk

Chief Executive: Juliet Rogers
Publishing Director: Kay Scarlett
Publisher: Jane Lawson

Design Manager: Vivien Valk
Design concept, art direction and design: Alex Frampton
Project Manager and Editor: Gordana Trifunovic
Production: Liz Malcolm
Photographer: Michele Aboud
Stylist: Sarah DeNardi
Food preparation: Mark Core

National Library of Australia Cataloguing-in-Publication Data
Broadhurst, Lucy. Ready, Steady, Party: Cooking for kids and with kids. Includes index.
ISBN 978 1 74196 449 3 (pbk.)
1. Cookery. Children's parties. 641.568

Printed by 1010 Printing International Limited in 2009. PRINTED IN CHINA.
The publisher and stylist would like to thank Jill Buckingham from www.sweetthemes.com.au for her wonderful cookie cutters.
Many thanks to our models Ava, Ruby, Tipani, Ellee, Elke, Milan, Mabel, Maggie and Mary.

IMPORTANT: Those who might be at risk from the effects of salmonella poisoning (the elderly, pregnant women, young children
and those suffering from immune deficiency diseases) should consult their doctor with any concerns about eating raw eggs.

CONVERSION GUIDE: You may find cooking times vary depending on the oven you are using. For fan-forced ovens,
as a general rule, set the oven temperature to 20°C (35°F) lower than indicated in the recipe. We have used 20 ml
(4 teaspoon) tablespoon measures.